# Adjudicating
# Theatre Performance:

## Responding to Competitions and Festivals

By Dean C. Slusser

**Dramatic Publishing**
Woodstock, Illinois • Australia • New Zealand • South Africa

# *** NOTICE ***

## COPYRIGHT LAW GIVES THE AUTHOR OR THE AUTHOR'S AGENT THE EXCLUSIVE RIGHT TO MAKE COPIES.

MMX by
DEAN C. SLUSSER

Printed in the United States of America
*All Rights Reserved*
(ADJUDICATING THEATRE PERFORMANCE:
Responding to Competitions and Festivals)

ISBN: 978-1-58342-692-0

# ACKNOWLEDGMENTS

I thank my editor and friend, Pat Whitton Forrest, for taking what I thought was a casual conversation in 2008 and inspiring me to turn it into a dream come true. Her encouragement, her guidance, her patience and her constant support all helped me make it through this process, but it is her exceptional gift for her craft for which I am most thankful. I could not have written this book without her, and I am thankful that God sent her across my path.

James Dodding, a friend and colleague for the past twenty years, is also due my appreciation. It is his teachings on which my entire philosophy of adjudication is founded.

I next thank Dr. Michael Richardson of Southeastern Louisiana State University for bringing me to the point in my career where, when I had the chance to write a book, I believed I could do it. Mike spent more than a decade as my mentor, and never gave up on me. I will always be grateful for our friendship.

Special thanks go to my friends Elaine Malone, Mary Norman and Scott McElheney, who had faith in my ability to do this thing and served as sounding boards off which I could bounce ideas. Our colleagues sustain us in our professional lives.

I must also thank Dr. Stan DeHart, who began as my friend but soon became an important mentor. Stan—you taught me that I have something to say, and that it might be worth hearing. I will always be grateful.

To Dr. Robert C. Hansen from the University of North Carolina at Greensboro, I also offer my heartfelt thanks. Bob was my undergraduate advisor at Bowling Green State University where I completed my bachelor's and master's degrees in theatre. I have told him often that my success is largely due to the training and guidance I received at BGSU.

Finally I offer my thanks and love to my wife, Susan, and my children, Stephanie, Phillip and Gabriel. Pretty darn much doesn't even come close!

And Mom—if you can hear me up there—I wrote a book!

"What families have in common around the world
is that they are the place where people learn
who they are and how to be that way."

–Jean Illsley Clarke

*This text is dedicated to two very special families
that equipped me to write it*

The Georgia Theatre Conference
The Southeastern Theatre Conference

*And to the two very dear friends
who brought me into those families*

Gerald Ray Horne
R. Lynn Wooddy

# TABLE OF CONTENTS

# INTRODUCTION

*"Everybody talks about the judging but nobody does anything about it."*

I have taught theatre for more than twenty-five years and directed in an educational setting for more than thirty. I have subjected a production cast and crew to the critical response of a panel of adjudicators nearly fifty times in my career. I have heard and read criticism by dozens of adjudicators about hundreds of productions, and I have responded to so many festivals and judged so many competitions that I have lost count. Every competition or festival I ever attended, adjudicated or participated in had one thing in common. *Some*one—often *everyone*—complained about the judging!

In 1989, I made the transition from college to high school teaching. I was familiar with one-act play festivals and had adjudicated several during the past five years. In the fall of this transition year, I had my first experience as the recipient of an adjudicator's critique.

I have always chosen plays that "spoke to me." In reading them, they would tell me how important they were. They would strike a chord with me. Such was the case with Jean Anouilh's *Antigone*, which had spoken to me, telling me that it was the next play I simply must produce. Unfortunately, the play told me I must direct it before I knew I was going to be doing it with high school students.

When I arrived in my first high school setting, my first production assignment was the Region One Act play competition. I mounted a production of *Antigone*, even though I had serious doubts about whether students at such a young age could grasp the meaning of the text or the symbolism of Anouilh's adaptation.

My doubts were unfounded. While the cast was young and completely inexperienced, they were among the most committed students I had ever had the pleasure of directing. They focused—sometimes intensely—on their search for understanding. They longed to please. I was pleasantly surprised and proud of the work they had done and the production they had put together.

## Preparing to be adjudicated

For our public performances we preset the stage, but the Georgia High School Association's one-act play competition rules dictated that our time limit was "bare stage to bare stage," so we rehearsed the load-in and strike between our public performances and our competition trip.

We were, of course, a young troupe, led by a young director who was participating in his first competition. In addition, because I believed that the educational experience should involve growing into higher levels of responsibility and achieving independence, I was not backstage with the students.

We had a lot to learn. My first lessons were that I should never approach the load-in for a competition play as something separate from the performance itself, I should always tend to little details like work lights, and my stage manager, rather than participating in the load-in, should be standing down center supervising it and making certain everything is done correctly. These lessons hit home—mercilessly—on a cool November morning at the Georgia Theatre Conference

Annual Festival of One Act Plays held that year in Augusta, when the lights came up.

My approach to setting the stage had been casual simply because it never occurred to me there might be a problem. The problem lay not with the cast and crew, but with me. I had not considered all of the possible obstacles to executing a smooth performance. In our home space, we had rehearsed under the faux darkness of midnight blue gels. I had not thought to appoint an overseer. Each student took on a specific task for pre-setting the show, As I preached so often in class and rehearsal, each student had learned what needed to be done, learned how to do it, and done it well.

At the competition in Augusta that November day, we did not realize that the facility in which we were performing did not have the midnight blue work lights that we practiced with back home. Since we did not consider the possibility, we did not prepare for the problem. When our lighting tech faded the stage to black for the set-up, he did not realize that the crew was in complete darkness. My students did their best, but had never entered the stage and found a need to rearrange the furniture. No one had ever experienced the need to stop a rehearsal over these kinds of problems so that they could fix them and continue. Consequently, no one did.

When the lights came up on our performance, the misplaced set pieces completely blocked the traffic patterns we had established for the show. Freestanding stair units that were supposed to sit left and right of center were too close to one another. Archways were out of place Furniture blocked planned crosses. It was not a pretty picture.

At rise, Antigone entered and stopped in her tracks (and in mid-sentence) only briefly when she realized she could not execute the blocking we had rehearsed. She recovered immediately, and adapted to the best of her ability. For the next forty-five minutes, I watched some of the most painful reworking of a play that I had ever witnessed as these dedicated young performers tried to maintain the integrity of their story in the very midst of not being able to tell it. Our beautiful, sometimes intricate stage pictures were gone. The composition was out of balance. The rhythm was off. Though they battled valiantly to get it back, they could not recover. It was my fault. I prepared them well for what was supposed to happen, but I had not prepared them at all for what *might* happen.

I pulled the cast and crew together quickly after the performance, and commended them for their composure in the face of major, serious complications. I told them I was proud, reminding them that they had done well the tasks I had asked them to do, and apologizing for not preparing them for the unexpected. They were okay. We were all okay. We were going to learn from our mistakes. We would fix this problem before the Georgia High School Association Region competition, and preparation for that event was, after all, the real reason we came to Augusta.

**Then the adjudicators came...**

I know there were three because in my 23-year history with Georgia Theatre Conference, they have always used three adjudicators. I only remember one individual, but I remember him vividly. He was the third judge—a local priest who taught in a nearby parochial school. He wore black slacks and a black shirt with a clerical collar under a well-worn tan corduroy blazer. The jacket highlighted the remaining color in his yellowed white hair and full beard, the latter so admirable that to this day I sometimes wonder if there is an Eastern Orthodox parochial school in Augusta.

We received our adjudication in the lobby of the theatre for that festival. The cast and crew stood in a large circle with the adjudicator of the moment standing in the center. It was in this setting that adjudicator number three, our bearded friend, walked over to within about a foot of the fourteen-year-old girl who played Antigone, tilted his head in a condescending fashion, peered at her from over his half-lenses and said "**You**... were ***not...interesting***!" He paused briefly for dramatic effect, then turned to the rest of the circle and continued his critique.

In thirty years of teaching, twenty-five years of directing and adjudicating, dozens of festivals and competitions and hundreds of productions, I can remember only one specific comment from an adjudicator and I remember it as clearly, as if it happened yesterday. I close my eyes and see him vividly.

"You...were ***not...interesting***!"

I am not sure my young Antigone ever completely recovered from the experience, and I know I did not, but as galling as his comment was, it was not what concerned me most. The truly offensive element of the critique is that it was a diatribe of value judgments that offered nothing constructive to cast, crew and director. I had brought my students to what I understood would be an educational experience that was not very educational—at least not in the sense I expected it to be.

## Why were we there?

This is an important question posed by James Dodding, an active member of the Guild of British Adjudicators whose training and friendship helped inspire me to write this book. He believed this question should be the driving force behind the work of every adjudicator: "If we do not provide an educational experience for competitors and audience, why are we there?"

Often I have wished that the bearded priest had asked himself that very question. It is ironic to me that on that November day our priestly adjudicator, though one might reasonably conclude he was interested in changing peoples' lives, changed a young life in ways that I can only hope were not intended. I wonder if he is even aware of his legacy.

Dodding closed every training session I ever worked with him by raising another question. This question was one that he answered, honestly, with each individual critique he offered those who went through his training: "Would you respect this adjudicator?"

He always closed his critiques of trainees' adjudication with a statement in answer to this question. When he closed his summary with the simple statement, "I would respect this adjudicator," it was high praise. Many thoughts, emotions, and reactions come to mind when I consider the only adjudicator comment I can remember verbatim in the past thirty years, but respect is not one of them.

## Accentuate the positive

Marketing research suggests that a customer will share a positive experience with as many as 25 people, and will share a negative experience with as many as 250 people. In that regard, I am human and am prone to share negative stories like the experience I had with *Antigone*. It is easy, and perhaps natural, to focus on the bad, but when I consider Dodding's question—"Would you respect this adjudicator?"—I must confess that I have witnessed and experienced infinitely more adjudicators who earned my respect than those who did not. My purpose in writing this book is not to attack people who are willing to share their knowledge, experience, passion and understanding of theatre in an effort to inspire and motivate others towards success. On the contrary, I want to celebrate effective adjudication, and encourage all adjudicators and respondents to adhere to a standard that promotes the development of theatre artists at every level.

For every negative story about an adjudication experience, I have countless positive stories. One of my favorites involved a guest director who prepared a one-act adaptation of *The Importance of Being Earnest* for our annual competition play. At one of the annual festivals in which we participated, the panel of judges was effusive in their praise for the production, and particularly for the young man who played Algernon. Comments concerning the work of the cast were as specific and focused as "Algernon was wonderfully over the top," and as broad and all encompassing as "a very nice job of ensemble acting—and a very nice job of catching the rather tipsy flavor of Wilde's play." Later in the festival, when one of the coordinators approached me to clarify the name of the actor playing Algernon, I suspected that some kind of recognition was afoot. In a money-saving effort, we had decided not to have the students stay for the awards banquet that year, so we implemented a scheme to arrange for a few students to stay, then made certain that our Algernon was among those present for the awards. That evening, he was named best actor in a festival of nearly 20 plays and 200 performers.

Our experience with Algernon was one of many over the years that resulted in recognition for individual performers as well as our ensemble, but in reflecting on the respect I have developed for adjudicators, most revealing is the number of times we did not receive special recognition but simply learned insights from their critiques that helped us to grow.

With warm regards and lifelong appreciation to James Dodding, I hope to provide adjudicators and respondents (and directors, students and audience members) with a model of assessment that establishes common ground in the content, approach and delivery of oral and written communication of a production critique in a festival or competition setting. I want all adjudicators to recognize that their role is not to entertain an audience of listeners with their witty observations; it is not to expound on their knowledge and experience as directing professionals; it is not even to pick a winner—any group of two or three individuals can do that. The role of the adjudicator is to turn a cast and crew's difficult and often negative experience of submitting their most personal work to the subjective criticism of three strangers into the positive and powerful experience of living the life of a student of theatre. I want the readers of this book to come away from it inspired to be, in Dodding's words, *respected* in their work, and to be worthy of that respect. In other words, I do not want just to complain about the judging. I want to do something about it.

# CHAPTER ONE

## Competition or Festival?

### The Roles of Adjudicator and Respondent

Theatre in western civilization was rooted in the competitive tradition of ancient Greece. The City Dionysia was a four-day theatre contest. On each of the first three days a playwright presented a trilogy of tragic plays. On the fourth day each playwright presented a satyr play. Winners were named. Prizes were given. Among the winners of the City Dionysia were Thespis, whom legend credits as being the first actor; Sophocles, who appears to have been the most prolific of the ancient Greek playwrights; and Euripides, who introduced the concept of melodrama into the theatre.

Today, tens of thousands of amateur performers across the United States participate every year in adjudicated performances of plays, whether they call them festivals or competitions, in a variety of performance settings that range from local, state and regional festivals for middle and high school students, to state, national and international festivals for community theatre groups, to performances at the college and university level for the Kennedy Center American College Theatre Festival. In some cases, these events are one-stop performances. In other situations, outstanding productions are selected for advancement to a more competitive level.

## The Role of Competition

The focus of this text is theatrical adjudication, but the concepts addressed in it are universal. All over the world, people are competing for prizes, and judges are deciding who gets them. We see it everywhere. Young women enter the pageant circuit from the local level to national and international events such as Miss America, Miss U.S.A. and Miss Universe. Athletes in a variety of settings compete not on the basketball court or football field where they score against one another, but on the diving platform, the ice rink, or the ski jump, where a panel of adjudicators uses subjective observations to determine the outcome. Even professional bull riding, billed as the most dangerous eight seconds in sports, relies first on the objective goal of whether the rider met the eight-second qualifying time, then on a panel of three judges who assign scores for both the rider and the bull.

The quest for the prize and the role of the judge in the process has permeated our popular culture with programs like *Dancing with the Stars*, *America's Got Talent*, and *American Idol*. Judges, who were invisible for years, have come to the forefront to become household names in these and similar settings. They have become celebrities in their own right, and their antics, however inappropriate in terms of professionalism or decorum, have helped to carry their programs to high ratings.

In our own lives, we have all had experience with adjudication, both formal and informal. When I was seven years old, a panel of high school girls selected me for three numbers in the neighborhood variety show they produced in our neighbor's garage. My fifth-grade teacher passed over me for the role of narrator in our school's Thanksgiving play and cast the principal's son instead. I recovered.

Adjudication is part of the world of performance, but it is part of the "real world," too. Ask any job applicant how the interview went and you will get a report about adjudicators. Car dealers are aware that customers evaluate their performance with every interaction. In each of these examples, and many from your life, we placed our fate, our future, and our self-esteem in the hands of others who were often strangers. How often was the experience a positive one, and how often did we walk away wishing that the adjudicators involved had been more respectful of the performers whose work they assessed? As different as these examples may seem, they all have some form of adjudication in common, and meaningful adjudication in any setting shares some common concepts and characteristics.

The focus of this text, then, is theatre adjudication, but the substance is about the human experience, the passion for learning, and the courage of artistry that prompts us—even impels us—to submit our work, our identity, and our sense of being, to the review of others.

## Can Competition Be Harmful?

In recent years, various advocates of theatre education have promoted an agenda that opposes theatre competitions. The strength of this philosophy ebbs and flows, and the arguments can digress to outright silliness. In my home state of Georgia, for example, we have five high school classifications based on size, and each classification is broken into eight regions. In each classification the winning play from each region advances to the state championship, so at the end of the cycle each year, we have five state champions—one in each classification. I remember attending a meeting where we considered a proposal to petition the state organization to change from a competition to a festival format. In the competitive format, plays are scored on a numerical system by three judges, and rankings are assigned. The top four places are recognized at both the region and the state levels. Competitions were harmful, proponents of the festival format argued, because too many people went home losers and not enough schools were recognized. When pressed for the details of how the proposed festival system would work, proponents said that instead of scores and rankings, judges would assign ratings of superior, excellent, good and fair in a fashion similar to that used in many music events in the state.

"Who moves on to the state level?" asked one director.

"The best play of the festival would go forward."

"But what if more than one school receives a superior rating?"

"The judges would pick the production that was best to move on."

"So instead of giving special recognition to four schools, we would only give it to one?"

The philosophy that theatrical competition is harmful for students is an extension of a similar argument in the education field. In at least one case the philosophy was taken to such an extreme that even auditions for a play could not be competitive. In 2008, a school production of *Snow White and the Seven Dwarfs* in Japan featured 25 Snow Whites, no dwarfs, and no wicked witch, the result of aggressive parents who eventually forced the school into admitting the injustice of selecting just one girl to play the title role.

There are, of course, valid considerations on both sides of the argument. The International Thespian Society (ITS) and its parent organization, the Educational Theatre Association (EdTA), tend to focus on non-competitive festivals, though many states implement a screening process of some kind to help balance the opportunities available to perform with the number of interested production teams. The Kennedy Center/American College Theatre Festival (KC/ACTF) format promotes a non-competitive philosophy, with festival participants, more often than not, producing in their home venues with guest respondents in attendance. These organizations have done tremendous work on behalf of educational theatre at the secondary and post-secondary levels. They are clearly successful, popular, and effective in promoting the value of non-competitive theatre. Still, I contend that healthy competition is also an effective catalyst for developing and sustaining educational theatre programs.

## The Benefits of Healthy Competition

Based on my experience as both competitor and adjudicator, I believe that the problems we often associate with competition are more reflective of the attitude of the participants than the structure or the inherent characteristics of the event itself. Unhealthy competition—as reflected in events where participants (directors, coaches, players) are obsessed with winning at any cost—is destructive and detrimental to the educational environment and the human spirit. Healthy competition is that in which each competitor respects the strengths and the talents of the other; healthy competition celebrates excellence in the same spirit reflected in the original City Dionysia or the original Olympic games; and healthy competition can effectively contribute to theatre programs in the educational setting.

### Competitions are attractive to students—they draw them in.

Twenty-six years in the classroom has taught me one thing above all else. Students are competitive. Competition is attractive not just to students, but to nearly all of us. Whether we are competitors or fans, we take competition seriously, and we are drawn to it. We like winners, and we like striving to be winners. In an era of intense focus on the need to connect with students and encourage them to complete educational programs, engaging in competition is another strategy to help students connect and motivate them to stay in school.

### Competitions prepare students to be competitive in the real world.

Regardless of a student's chosen field of endeavor, competition helps to prepare him for the competition he will face in the real world: competition for and at work, in social settings, and in other concerns of life. The competitive spirit motivates success in all areas of life. Competition may need to be balanced by professionalism, but it provides a tremendous opportunity to help prepare students for a bright future.

**Competitions help to promote high school theatre programs.**

Like students, teachers, administrators, alumni and members of the community understand competition. The competitive teams in the school are among the most visible manifestations of the educational system in any community. The competitive event is news in itself, and provides opportunities for local newspaper coverage and other public relations strategies. The public relations opportunity doubles when the team brings home a trophy. These events and achievements speak to the community and build support in fans and in contributions. People like success. They support success. And, as even those teams who come home without placing in the competition have learned, people support competitors who strive for success.

What are we teaching our students if we pretend that the world is just, or that it is not competitive in nature? More importantly, the adjudication process, and the adjudicator's role, whether we call the performances festivals, showcases or competitions, is basically the same.

# CHAPTER TWO

## An Adjudicator's Role

The purpose of any adjudication is to comment, objectively and constructively, in an experienced, sympathetic, sensitive and specific way on all aspects of the production. To facilitate the discussion of these attributes, I will use the adjudicator reported in the introduction as a frame of reference.

### Objective Commentary: *Maintain an aesthetic distance.*

Our sample adjudicator's first mistake was that he abandoned objectivity and aesthetic distance in his delivery. Both physically and emotionally, he made it personal. A professional adjudicator should deliver objective responses to cast, crew and audience. These responses should be in the form of observations and should remain relatively formal. They may include personal reactions to the adjudicator's observations, but should never include value judgments. This distinction is often difficult for inexperienced adjudicators to discern. "You were not interesting" is a value judgment. By making the statement, the adjudicator first assumed the authority to make decisions about what is and is not interesting, and then imposed his conclusions on everyone who saw the play. He presented his conclusion as a fact of the situation when the only verifiable fact was that *this adjudicator* found the character uninteresting.

The adjudicator could have made his point in a variety of ways while still maintaining the aesthetic distance and professional demeanor appropriate to his position. He might have said any one of a number of things including, but not limited to:

"The actress playing Antigone…

> …did not appear to take the stage when she entered;

> …did not exude the authority appropriate to her character's position;

> …seemed hesitant in her delivery (or her actions)."

These suggestions do not disqualify the adjudicator from making "I" statements. On the contrary, the adjudicator is there to respond, has been asked to respond, and should respond, with his personal reactions. Personal responses, though, implicitly if not explicitly, should remain exclusively the property of the adjudicator and not promote an assumption of omnipotence. An adjudicator who leans towards the use of "I" might have delivered the same basic message, while still communicating a sense of his exclusive ownership of the conclusions he offered. In this vein, he might have said:

"I did not see an appropriate depth of character in Antigone."

"I thought that Antigone's character was a little two-dimensional."

"I wanted to see a stronger emotional commitment from Antigone."

or even:

"I found myself wanting the character of Antigone to be more interesting."

The examples above still reflect the personal reactions of the speaker (or writer) but do not make broad-based conclusions as if they are statements of fact. The adjudicator in these examples makes it clear that the observations are personal, and not conclusive. There is no suggestion of judgment. The role of the adjudicator is to share with the audience what he or she *observed.* An effective adjudicator reports those observations and his reaction to them objectively, without prejudice or judgment. The ultimate judgment as to the value of a production rests with the audience, not with the respondent.

**Constructive Commentary:** *Provide suggestions for improvement.*

Our sample adjudicator's second mistake was his failure to offer any correction in connection with the judgment he passed on the young actress playing Antigone. There was nothing constructive in his comment. This problem is among the most consistent sources of frustration for directors and actors who submit their work to adjudication. Many adjudicators seem to think that the purpose of the adjudication is to tell the director what is wrong with the production. Directors leave the adjudication with a clear understanding that the adjudicator did not care for the production, but with no idea what to do to fix it. In fairness, this approach to adjudication is due, at least in part, to the very terms we use. An adjudicator is, by definition, a judge, and a judge, by definition, passes judgment. The tendency to tear down a production rather than to build up a team is particularly prevalent in settings where numerical scores and formal scoring forms are used. All too often, an adjudicator will take points off with no written explanation as to why he deducted them. In the context of educational theatre, it is appropriate for the adjudicator to share the results of his study and to explain how he arrived at his settlement. Indeed, even in the legal setting judges often explain how they arrive at their decision. Directors understand that when an actual scoring system is used, the adjudicator will deduct points, but would like to know the thinking of the judge. At least one definition of adjudicator suggests that he or she "studies and settles." By following the legal model, theatre adjudicators have an opportunity to enhance the experience of the performing company.

As problematic as a formal scoring system with written scores can be, directors can be equally frustrated, or more so, when they perform in a setting where no formal scoring system is used and the adjudicators deliver an oral critique. The Georgia Theatre Conference has used this approach in their annual secondary school one-act play festivals for decades. Three adjudicators take five minutes each following each performance to share their observations with the cast and crew. They may or may not provide written notes to the directors at the end of the festival. Because of time constraints and a genuine (and admirable) desire to encourage young performers, these critiques tend to be predominantly positive with few if any constructive criticisms. As a result, many companies in the festival leave the adjudication feeling very optimistic about their chances of winning Best Play or Runner Up—the only two overall production awards mandated by the festival rules. Obviously, nearly all of the teams are disappointed at the end of the festival. They walk away from the awards ceremony wondering what they could have done wrong, and why the adjudicators forgot to mention the problems with their show. Adjudication can be and should be an uplifting and educational experience for the participants. In order for that to happen, the adjudicator must be ready to make constructive suggestions for improvement.

Consider for a moment how we determine credibility in a speaker. When the speaker is someone known to the audience, his record of accomplishment probably speaks to credibility. Someone less known may share a little of his or her background as a means of establishing an initial sense of credibility. Ultimately, though, the audience will assess credibility based on what the speaker has to say. If a speaker makes observations and comments that suggest a thoughtful response, if he demonstrates an understanding of the complexity of the topic addressed, if he speaks from an informed perspective, the audience will listen and respect what he has to say. This observation brings us to the third mistake on the part of our sample adjudicator in the introduction to the text. His choice to abandon aesthetic distance and engage in generally destructive criticism left him with a lack of credibility. He lost respect as soon as he made such a rash conclusion for both the lack of professionalism and the lack of knowledge he displayed. To effectively illustrate this point, I set aside the adjudicator's story and go back to my own childhood.

As a child, not unlike my experience as an adult, there were words in the lexicon that I simply did not use. At best, using these words could result in being ignored. At worst, they could lead to being reprimanded—perhaps even soundly rapped—for my impertinence. Such words and phrases might be categorized as inappropriate, disrespectful, or perhaps even vulgar. Educated people, respectful people, informed people, did not use these words. Two that come to mind immediately are "shut up" and "jerk," but there were other words as well. Some words were distasteful; others were hurtful, and still others were just plain "bad," but all of these kinds of words had one thing in common. They reflected more on the speaker than on the intended target. People who used them were unimaginative, disrespectful, and generally uninformed. Admirable people, deserving of respect, simply did not use them.

I believe that "you…were not…interesting" may fall in the category of these undesirable words. They were distasteful. They were hurtful. They offered nothing productive.

Adjudicators should share their thoughts from an informed perspective. Their commentary should reflect an understanding of what the theatre is about. The observations they present, and the manner in which they present them, should exude a message of knowledge of the subject matter and respect for the efforts of the participants. The adjudicator, in other words, may legitimately reference his own experience as part of his critique. The danger for adjudicators comes when they allow the response to a production to digress to a litany of "should have dones." The adjudicator's job is not to tell the company what he or she would have done, but to *respond* and *react* in an informed way to what *they* did.

**Sympathetic Commentary:** *Be sensitive to the people of the play.*

Our sample adjudicator's most egregious error may have been to show no regard or compassion for the people whose work he reviewed. The company of actors and technicians who shared their work for review was worthy of respect and deserving of recognition of the effort they put forth in the production. By presenting their work for adjudication, they intentionally let their guard down and exposed themselves to harm. In one sense, the relationship is not unlike that between a doctor and patient. The patient exposes all—sometimes literally—and trusts the physician to respond in a clinical and professional manner. Participants working with an adjudicator exhibit a similar level of trust. They are reasonable to expect a level of clinical professionalism similar to what a physician might practice. A doctor makes emotionally charged statements in a calm, unemotional manner to reduce the anxiety of the patient. He does not make the conversation personal. It is neither about him nor about the patient. On the contrary, the physician reports to the patient concerning his examination and the findings that resulted from the examination. An adjudicator should take note of this kind of bedside manner. Adjudication is not personal. It is neither about the adjudicator, nor about the performer. It is a report on the observations recorded by the adjudicator and the findings that resulted and nothing more. By saying "you were not interesting…" the sample adjudicator's comment was personal, perhaps even insulting. He made the critique not about the production and his observations, but about the actress who played the part. He passed merciless judgment on her in front of her peers, teachers and parents. His delivery, walking directly up to her and gazing over the top of his half-lenses, was condescending. His impact on her was crushing.

The adjudicator has an obligation to be honest, but in the midst of his honesty he must be sensitive to and respectful of the vulnerability of the performers and technicians in the company. To be truly effective he must also be sympathetic to the company in the context of the work its members set out to do.

One component of adjudicating a diving competition, as well as some other sports, is the degree of difficulty. In most adjudicated festivals, the level of difficulty does not appear as a formal element of the scoring system or response. The adjudicator may or may not take into account the special challenges of a given selection, but all too often responses focus on production values that do not consider the level of the challenge. Consequently, well-done plays with little theatrical or literary substance outperform classics and other more challenging pieces nobly attempted by participants.

The opportunity to incorporate a selection's degree of difficulty into the formal scoring process may be limited by the rules of a festival, but the adjudicator can always acknowledge the noble ambition of a participating company in written and spoken commentary, even if the recognition cannot be immediately translated into scores. Similarly, companies that mount productions of "lesser" plays and do so effectively might be encouraged by an adjudicator to raise the bar and attempt a more demanding piece.

## Specific Commentary: *Avoid generalizations.*

Inexperienced adjudicators, sometimes even experienced ones, often draw conclusions without any explanation or evidence to defend their statements. Their behavior in this regard suggests—or at least implies—that they exude such expertise that they need not support their conclusions. Directors and others who submit their work to adjudication find the omission of specific information to support the adjudicators' observations to be one of the most frustrating aspects of submitting their work for review.

Adjudicators are not forbidden to make general comments as part of a critique, but an effective adjudicator makes every effort to provide specific examples to illustrate his point. In order to be truly effective, an adjudicator should immediately follow any general comment with one or two specific examples from the play to illustrate the point. For all of the concern expressed about the need to recognize the vulnerability and be sensitive to the people of the play, a production company can be really quite resilient when a response to their performance is honest and includes specific information to support the response.

The effective adjudicator, then, should deliver commentary that is **objective, constructive, experienced, sympathetic** and **specific**. These qualities are common characteristics of a respected adjudicator. They are worthy goals for anyone who desires to respond effectively to a theatre performance.

## Developing a Vocabulary for Dramatic Criticism

Some words, phrases and perspectives do not belong in the vocabulary of a professional adjudicator. The same observation is probably true in any profession—from the politician's "I cannot recall," to the reporter's "past history." For the theatre adjudicator, the inappropriate comments fall into two or three categories: value judgments, entertaining quips, and "when I did this play…"

## Value Judgments

An adjudicator cannot depend on general value judgments to facilitate his response to the performance of a play. While it is entirely appropriate to make observations about the performance and to use those observations, at times at least, to address the adjudicator's perceptions or reactions to specific moments in the play, it is wrong for him make general conclusions or judgments of value in a manner to suggest the he speaks for the audience. Among the most common traps that lead to value judgments is the use of superlatives in adjudication. Adjudicators know that they are there to encourage performers, directors and technicians in their endeavors. It may seem to them that a little hyperbole does not hurt the effort, and yet it can lead to difficult misunderstandings when "the best," "the highest," "the most colorful production I have seen" fails to gain recognition in the final standings. Neither should the adjudicator use superlatives in the negative sense. No company wants to go home with the distinction of being the "least" or the "worst" production in any category!

Another problem with using value judgments as an adjudication tool is that they are simply not very helpful in the educational process. An adjudicator may thrill a company or actor by showering praise about how good—or great—they were, but in the end, these students of theatre have gained nothing useful if they do not understand what they did that prompted the conference of value on their performance.

## Entertaining Quips

Adjudicators who depend on value judgments may be playing God without realizing it. All too often, festival judges or respondents act as if it is their job to entertain the audience with witty observations about a performance—often made at the expense of the performers or technicians involved. We have all seen the type. They pepper their comments with punch lines, showing no respect or compassion for the company that is the subject, and sometimes the victim, of their observations. At best, they come across as unfocused, unprofessional, and occasionally incompetent judges who do not understand the difference between an adjudicator and a critic.

## "When I Did This Play…"

The final, and most offensive, category of responses that professional adjudicators should avoid is any statement that begins with "When I did this play," whether the reference involves acting, designing, directing, or some other element of production. It is most often seen in public comments about the performance. Such situations are offensive enough, but occasionally the attitude manifests itself behind the scenes and threatens the integrity of a contest or festival.

I took part adjudicating a recent contest where three judges independently selected their top choices for recognition and submitted them to the coordinator for tabulation. Once we submitted our results, we were asked to engage in discussions to select candidates to receive acting awards. In the discussion of candidates for best actor, I believed there to be only one viable candidate. One colleague, a college professor, agreed with my observation. The third judge, however, was hesitant to agree, and asked us to consider other possibilities. We told him we were willing to hear his suggestions, but were somewhat taken aback when his suggested alternates had submitted notably less substantive performances. In the ensuing conversation, he explained that his problem with the actor we had chosen was that he was currently directing the same play, and had a very different interpretation from the one the actor in the competition had pursued. Ultimately, we overruled him and he conceded to our recommendations, but the entire incident tarnished the reputation of the adjudicator, and it got worse. Later, when the final standings had been tabulated and we were able to review one another's rankings and compare notes, we learned that the play that one colleague and I placed first was assigned a third place ranking by the third adjudicator. The play was the one that featured the recipient of the best acting award—the play that our fellow adjudicator was directing at the time—and he placed it third not because of the quality of the performance, but because he disagreed with the director's interpretation, regardless of how successful the director was in realizing it. I found the entire experience beyond distasteful and can no longer respect him as an adjudicator or an educator.

If value judgments, entertaining quips, and "when I did this play" are all pitfalls that adjudicators should avoid, then what is the substance of an effective adjudication? The adjudicator should guide his commentary with observations that include personal responses, specific details, and respectful commentary.

## Personal Responses

The adjudicator should build his remarks around honest, personal reactions to a performance. The individual responding to a play was not invited to the event because of something he is not. He was asked to participate because of who he _is_. Many adjudicators seem to forget this basic concept. When asked to adjudicate a contest or festival they seem to think they are expected to be someone or something different from what they are. The resulting commentary is often pretentious and the commentator overwhelmed with self-importance.

All any director wants an audience to do is react honestly to the performance. They want the same honest reaction from the adjudicator. Effective adjudicators begin the experience like any other member of the audience. They suspend their disbelief; they immerse themselves in the imaginary world of the play; and they react, honestly, to the story the company is telling. Their response, then, becomes a discussion of their theatrical experience—a report on the "magic of the play" as they experienced it. They comment on what they found to be exciting, suspenseful, and well done. And yes, they comment on what confused them, what they did not understand, and what they found to be ineffective. These statements are not value judgments like the ones discussed earlier in this chapter. They are _personal_ responses made in a public forum. This opportunity for public commentary is what sets the adjudicator's experience apart from the regular audience, but it comes with additional responsibilities.

## Specific Details

Because of the awesome power an adjudicator wields, he must be ever conscious of how he explains or supports his observations. Many adjudicators make a common mistake of sharing the observations without providing the supporting details in spoken or written commentary. A performance group can find this kind of adjudication anywhere from mildly unfulfilling to entirely frustrating To avoid this pitfall, an adjudicator must include specific details to support and explain each of the observations he makes in the adjudication.

Let us consider an example of a positive comment that might be delivered in a critique:

"The party scene was outstanding!"

Or another:

"I liked the actor who portrayed the killer in your play."

In each of these examples, the company is initially going to have a positive response. The adjudicator complimented the company—collectively and individually—for their work. Unfortunately, though, it is a temporary euphoria at best, because at some point after the commentary, the actors and technicians are going to realize that they do not know what they did well to evoke such a response in the adjudicator, and therefore they do not know what it is that they need to continue doing. The adjudicator should follow each of these comments with specific examples from the play, explaining what he saw and heard, and how his reaction to these things led to the observation he shared.

"I thought the party scene was outstanding because of the extent to which the characters on stage engaged one another. For example, when Sharon pulled the blond girl to the down right corner and told her secret, the party continued as any party would, with no one taking notice of the dialogue between the two. And the expression on the girl's face when Sharon told her was well-timed and consistent with how I think I would react if I were hearing such news."

Or: "I liked the actor who portrayed the killer in your play. He demonstrated a wonderful sense of detail—not just in his own work as an actor, but in his character's work relating to others in the play. He seemed almost paranoid at times, as if he were always spying on others, making mental notes.

The revised commentary in the first example also corrected another problem. "Outstanding" is a value judgment. The adjudicator's comment implies that according to some external, unknown, and very likely arbitrary standard, the work of these performers in their party scene met the criteria to qualify as "outstanding." The comment provides a vivid illustration of the fine line between appropriate and inappropriate responses. Adjudicators have the right and the responsibility to assign value to what they see, but they must also own that value, making clear to the performers and audience that the reaction is theirs and not universal in nature.

## Respectful Commentary

Finally, include only respectful commentary. This admonition does not preclude what a company might interpret as a negative observation or a constructive criticism. Respectful commentary in this context means that the adjudicator is always mindful of the weapons he wields and the harm he can do with them. *It is never the goal of an adjudicator to do harm*, and no effective adjudicator would ever intentionally do so.

I have known and watched adjudicators who have considered their work witty, entertaining, and expert. Respondents who fit these characteristics have one thing in common. They think the adjudication process is about *them* when in fact it is about the *production*. In the adjudication process, a company of actors and technicians places its most precious creation in the hands of a stranger. It is the responsibility of the stranger to treat the creation, and the creators, with care and respect, supporting them through what can at times be a difficult process while still introducing them to the things of the world they need to know. This need for respectful commentary is among the most important issues that face theatre adjudication. Participants in the process must understand the awesome responsibility, and the awesome opportunity, they are being offered when they are asked to respond to a performance.

### Reviewer, Dramaturge, and Adjudicator

In assessing the role of the adjudicator, it is helpful to acknowledge what he is not. His task is to inform, but he is not a reviewer/critic or a dramaturge. His role is also to inform, but the similarities stop when you scratch the surface of the comparison.

The reviewer provides information to the readers of his newspaper or website or television audience about how they should spend their entertainment dollars. In this sense, he is a consumer advocate rather than a production advocate. His relationship to the cast and production team is often non-existent and, in terms of professional ethics, probably should be. Rather than being accountable to the performers, he is accountable to his editors and his readers, who become the students in his attempt to educate individuals about the value of the production.

The dramaturge also provides information, but largely the focus of dramaturgy is to provide that information within the circle of the production. While the dramaturge may prepare a lobby display or a program note to help the audience better understand the theatrical experience, his primary work is done within the production process, giving directors, actors, and other members of the production team a better understanding of the historical content and references in the play. The work of the dramaturge is more directly educational than that of the reviewer, but the target students for this teacher are members of the production team, and the content is historical context.

In contrast to the reviewer and the dramaturge, the adjudicator is a provider of information about the production, whose commitment is not to his readers and whose content is not history. Like the reviewer, the adjudicator's work involves assessing and reporting on the value of the production, but his criteria differs from that used for a theatre review. The adjudicator's work is purely educational. He observes the choices made by members of the production team and the execution of those choices. His duty is to encourage and inspire. His delivery may be somewhat clinical in comparison to the flamboyant style of the theatrical reviewer. His immediate students are the people of the production, but he often acknowledges and includes the audience in his remarks. They are not intended to advise patrons on whether to buy a ticket for a show, but to share with the production team an analysis of their creative work.

# CHAPTER THREE

## Moving Toward Greater Professionalism

The story of my first foray into the world of one-act play festivals is not unique to the high school drama teacher. Hundreds of thousands of performers and directors from across the country, from every spectrum of theatre regularly participate in festivals and competitive events. While directors, casts and crews come to these events with varied backgrounds, abilities, and levels of experience, they all tend to leave with at least one common experience—at some point during the festival, they wondered if the judges were in their right minds.

They may have been offended by something as small as a comment made directly to a cast member, or as large as the final standings. It could involve a single responder, or an entire panel of judges. It might occur because the competition was obviously rigged, but it could also happen in the most honest and upright festival settings where the outcome was exactly as it should be. In general, the one thing that all directors know before they even get to the competition is that there are going to be problems with the judges. An adjudication without controversy is the exception—not the rule.

You might think that with such widespread discontent, directors would mount a grassroots campaign to improve the quality and professionalism of adjudication, but history and personal experience suggest otherwise. While most organizations that sponsor play festivals and competitions provide guidelines to the respondents and many offer some sort of orientation, few offer a formal certification process for adjudicators. This training element, by necessity, is a key component in any attempt to introduce standards of professional practice into the adjudication process.


## Training To Be a Professional

*Professionalism* is the word we use to describe *professionals*, who in turn are members of a *profession*. These terms, in the order listed, are progressively more limited in their interpretation. While "professionalism," for example, has a number of applied meanings in reference to an individual's conduct, appearance, or demeanor, "professional" is somewhat more limiting. We most often use the term as an adjective to describe an individual's behavior in a business relationship, or as a noun in reference to an individual whose position, knowledge base or expertise in a given field justify a higher level of recognition. "Profession," in turn, almost exclusively describes a group of individuals with specific characteristics. It has been argued that characteristics of a profession include autonomy; a clearly defined, highly developed, specialized, and theoretical knowledge base, control of training, certification, and licensing of new entrants; self-governing and self-policing authority, especially with regard to professional ethics; and a commitment to public service. It takes only a moment to review these traits and recognize what stands between play evaluation and a more professional approach. Adjudicators can certainly claim autonomy; no one would argue that they have a highly developed, specialized and theoretical knowledge base. Most, if not all, demonstrate a clear commitment to public service and the greater good. But the "profession" of adjudication lacks control of training and licensing, self-governance, and self-policing authority—at least in the United States.

## The British Model

There is, however, a model that can help us. The British Guild of Drama Adjudicators (GoDA) was founded in 1947 to "improve the standards of adjudication of amateur drama by establishing recognised principles of practice." Members are selected for invitation to the guild after a program of "instructing and testing candidates for membership in the nature and method of adjudication." All guild members are bound by strict rules of professional etiquette. The objectives of the Guild are:

1. *To supply qualified adjudicators to all organisations promoting amateur drama.*

2. *To enable its members to work unfettered towards the objectives of the Guild.*

3. *To provide opportunities for the discussion of the problems of adjudication and tuition either by schools, conferences, or by other means.*

The organization's website offers a thorough discussion of the rigorous expectations associated with selection for membership. Their discussion concerning the background and experience of guild members appears below:

*All candidates for membership are required to have professional or amateur stage experience (preferably both) and to possess a thorough knowledge of drama. A report upon each candidate is made to the Council of the Guild by an Approved Board on which there is at least one person who is not an adjudicator. New members are normally admitted as associate members for a period of two years during which time they will be advised by a mentor. They may be admitted to full membership after they have adjudicated no fewer than six Festivals during that time. Their admission will be at the discretion of the Council and based upon confidential reports from two festival organisers by whom the Associate Member has been employed, and an appraisal by a full member of the Guild. The responsibilities of associate members are the same as those of full members.*

*All members and associates are bound to observe certain minimum conditions of engagement. As the Guild is not an agency, negotiations for engagements must be made direct with the adjudicator, but the Guild will provide information and assistance to festival organisers.*

*All members of the Guild are bound to abide by the rules of any festival at which they undertake to adjudicate, and disciplinary action may be taken by the Council against any member who fails to do so.*

*More than eighty per cent of members of the Guild have had professional stage experience as actors, directors, or stage managers. Some are still engaged in the professional theatre, many of them highly distinguished members of the profession. All have experience of the conditions under which amateur plays are performed and are interested in the furtherance of amateur drama. Many are engaged in some form of teaching theatre. The ability to impart instruction, as well as sound judgment, is regarded as a necessary qualification for membership of the Guild.*

*Persons with knowledge of the stage and of drama, especially those who have had some experience of adjudication, are invited to apply for membership. Most members of the Guild are willing to adjudicate at verse-speaking festivals and to lecture on drama and various aspects of theatrical art. Members are also available for engagements as producers of plays, operas and musicals. In the event of an adjudicator being required to cancel at short notice, the services of the Guild are available.*

*The Guild is always ready to discuss any problems with festival organizers and to give them any advice or assistance in its power.*

The Guild prints a directory of its members for festival organizers who are advised to attend as many festivals and to hear as many adjudicators as possible.

### Can We Do This in the United States?

The policies of the Guild of Drama Adjudicators make it clear that adjudication is taking on the air of a profession in Great Britain. The guild's policies provide us with a model to pursue in the United States. The unanswered question, however, is whether we can create such a model. It's also whether we want to do so. At one time, I thought we did. Now I am not so sure.

In the early 1990s I served as chair of the Secondary School One Act Play Festival for the Southeastern Theatre Conference. GoDA member James Dodding was recommended as an adjudicator for our festival, and he graciously accepted. I was impressed with his content, delivery and style, and subsequently asked him to conduct an adjudicator training workshop at the next year's convention. I participated in the training program and immediately became hooked on the British approach. Equipped and ready to spread the gospel of adjudication, I set out to deliver adjudicator training sessions across the Southeast. I proposed the creation of a certification process that would help to guarantee our students would receive consistently professional responses steeped in meaningful educational experience and the world would be a better place.

As it turned out, I offended some people. At thirty years old, I was not quite the expert I had imagined myself to be. I was, in fact, perceived as a young upstart telling veteran adjudicators—some twice my age or older—what they needed to do. I had never even gotten a play through the screening process. Who was I to tell them what they needed to do?!? Their reaction was completely honest, but only partially correct.

Then, as now, there were many practicing adjudicators with a wealth of experience and a track record of professionalism. While they very well could have benefited from formal training and certification, they accomplished a great deal and built tremendous reputations without it. The implementation of adjudicator training programs would have to provide a procedure for recognizing those individuals in the field who already met the criteria for certification without the formal training. In this sense, critics of my adjudication crusade of nearly twenty years ago were correct. But in another sense their premise was false.

Those "veteran" adjudicators who opposed my proposals were also directors who would leave our festival and competition settings complaining about the judges—judges who met the same criteria as themselves! If the source of our complaint is that our students are getting neither a fair shake nor a valid educational experience, then we are committed educators and artists striving for the best possible opportunities for our students. If, on the other hand, we are complaining because the judges did not pick our production to win, or we disagreed with what they decided, we are little more than self-absorbed hypocrites who look for scapegoats on which to place the blame for our own failures.

Our dilemma is fairly clear. We often react with frustration to the responses of adjudicators in the theatre festivals in which we participate, but if we make an effort to improve the process, we all must be ready to commit to the changes that occur. We must submit ourselves to the training and certification requirements we impose on others. If we want to advance our craft of adjudication to a more professional level, we must police ourselves and one another. I am not sure that this goal is within reach, but I do believe that through a voluntary system of adjudicator training and certification we can have a grassroots impact on the role and conduct of theatre evaluators by offering a simple service—access to better, more professional adjudicators at every level. Our success depends on our ability to create and promote a universal framework for meaningful evaluation of plays. By "universal," I mean a framework that is useful to every level of educational and amateur theatre production—one which provides effective guidelines for the individual judging the high school play contest, the community theatre competition, and the university theatre festival alike. By "meaningful evaluation," I mean a framework that offers a valid learning experience where adjudicator, performer and audience can develop and implement a common vocabulary in discussions of the logistics and aesthetics of theatre performance—a learning laboratory where students of theatre from any age, experience level or walk of life can come away from the experience a more insightful artist. The creation and implementation of such a framework may seem a lofty goal, indeed, but it is within our reach if we choose to pursue it.

# CHAPTER FOUR

## The Content of Adjudication

In my quarter century of experience with adjudication models and philosophies, I always come back to James Dodding when I consider what items or areas to address in an adjudicator's response. When asked about the content of adjudication—what should be addressed?—Dodding, citing his British training, would plainly say "everything." He argued, and the British model reflects, that every element of a production warrants commentary. This position is not necessarily prevalent in the educational field. For example, the rules of the Georgia High School Association, and many other state organizations that sponsor the annual high school one-act play competition for most public and some private schools, make it very clear that the competition is an acting competition. Sets, costumes and other production values appear, if somewhat vaguely, in a section of the scoring sheet called "overall effect" and may be valued at only ten points on a one-hundred-point scale. Many participants in the competition setting, especially schools with larger student populations, travel to the event with elaborate, enormous sets, but if adjudicators adhere strictly to the guidelines published by the sponsor, these production values have little impact on the final standings.

Dodding was adamant in his opposition to the notion of a theatrical production's scoring or adjudication based on being "strictly an acting competition." To illustrate his point with training session participants, he once cited a production where one of the characters wore a pair of tie-dyed tennis shoes.

"Someone," he said, "worked hard to find or to create those shoes. You may choose to overlook them. You may argue that they did not contribute to the production. You may even conclude that the shoes are unimportant," he went on. "But they were important to someone—they were important to the young person who found them. They were important to the director who asked for them, to the actor who wore them, and to the company whose play benefited from the commitment and perseverance of the young man or woman who brought them to the production!" Dodding believed that adjudication should address every element of a production, and that a responsible, professional adjudicator was morally obligated to do just that.

The British model of adjudication breaks these production elements into four basic areas: stage presentation, production, acting, and endeavor. Each of these areas includes subdivisions that, combined, provide an opportunity for adjudication to include nearly every element of a theatre performance.

## Stage Presentation

In the British system, "stage presentation" includes setting, costumes, props, lighting, sound effects and music. A complete adjudication should respond to each of these areas to the extent that they are part of a given production. Setting addresses the set and other scenic elements of the play. Along with costumes and lighting, setting should be consistent with the production concept, appropriate to the period in which the play is set, and generally supportive of the theatrical experience. The role of the adjudicator is not to pass judgment on these choices based on whether he likes or dislikes them, but to assess the impact the choices had on the production. Similarly, sound effects and music, as appropriate, should support the overall concept and mood of the play. Responsibility for each of these elements of a production falls to individuals or groups of individuals on a production team, and each individual or group deserves a mention in the response. A thorough adjudicator would include an assessment—at least a comment or nod to each of these elements of stage presentation.

## Production—and the Role of the Director

The British definition of "production" includes the spirit or meaning of the play, the sense of teamwork, the pace and tempo of the performance, the stage pictures, and the overall telling of the story. Many of these areas involve the director's leadership and the production team's ability to jell as a unit.

The work of the director warrants consideration, not in terms of how to direct the play or how someone thinks it should have been directed, but in the context of what the adjudicator looks for and how he recognizes it. In my own experience, I tend to notice the work of the director in four areas: stage pictures and movement, striking moments, the sense of the whole, and casting.

In my responses to production, I am completely comfortable addressing the first three concerns. While I address the fourth concern at times, I tend to do so only with positive comments, and even then with caution.

**Stage pictures and movement** are primarily the responsibility of the director who, with his design team, views the production process from the perspective of the audience. The adjudicator assesses whether the stage remains in balance as well as the effects of an imbalanced stage. Do such effects contribute to the play or the scene? Do they ensure that all the audience can witness the action of the play? These issues are valid concerns for the adjudicator.

More often than not, I credit **striking moments**—those special scenes or moments in a performance—to the director's work. Even when the creative spark that discovers or creates those moments comes from the work of actors or technicians, it is the director who recognizes and exploits the opportunity. This, too, is an appropriate concern for the adjudicator to address.

The third production element that I tend to credit to the director is the **sense of the whole**. The director is ultimately responsible for everything that goes on stage. If the director is effective, the "everything" will become "one thing." An effective production flows from beginning to end, a single entity, a unity full and complete within itself. While technical elements, acting ensemble, and other factors may impact success, it is the director who is responsible for preparing production and creating the theatrical experience.

**Casting** is a difficult issue for the adjudicator for a variety of reasons. Commentary that challenges casting decisions, however accurate it may be, is not appropriate to the educational purpose and philosophy of the adjudication process.

This caution does not mean that an adjudicator should avoid honest assessment of an actor's individual performance. But to address casting as an issue can be too easily interpreted as calling into question whether the performer should even have been given the opportunity to play the role. Such speculation is helpful to neither the director nor the production team, and may be unbearably hurtful to the actor in question. It does nothing good, and should not be part of theatrical adjudication.

The British model includes **team work** as a production element, which is related to, but different from "spirit and meaning of the play," in the production section, or "overall impact or impression," discussed later as endeavor. As a production element, team work speaks to the company's ability to bring the spirit of the story to life. In the United States we often call it "ensemble." It is among the greatest contributors to an effective performance. Our perceptions of individual performers are often influenced by our perception of the amount of work they appear to put into a performance, compared to the quality of the outcome. In other words, that which we perceive to be "good acting," like good figure skating, good diving, or even good bull riding, appears to be as effortless as it is powerful. The same principle is true when we evaluate group performance, but the variables and the degree of difficulty increase according to the number of people in a scene or play. The audience is genuinely willing to suspend its belief, and does so enthusiastically, until something jars them back to reality, pulling them out of the illusion of the play. An effective ensemble creates the impression that their work is so effortless it is natural. The ensemble performance lulls the audience into an even deeper illusion. If the ensemble is weak, the play becomes choppy and awkward. As a result, the audience notices how hard the team is working, which in turn pulls them out of the illusion of the play.

Pace and tempo are references to the movement of the dialogue. **Pace**, specifically, might be described as the distance between the lines of dialogue (as opposed to rate, which references the distance between words in an actor's speech). The **tempo** of a production is movement of the story, the rise and fall of the action and dialogue. Stage pictures, or stage composition, address the visual balance of the staging. Is the picture on stage balanced? Are players clearly visible? Is the eye of the audience drawn to the appropriate focal point? Finally, the production category includes the telling of the story. Every play is written to tell a story to the audience, but some productions fail to achieve that goal. The adjudicator must ultimately make an assessment—has the company succeeded in telling the playwright's story?

## Acting

The acting portion of an adjudicator's task includes comments on characterization, projection, diction, expression, gesture, and movement. The actor's individual characterization is perhaps his greatest single contribution to the play. The depth of character, the believability the actor achieves and the compassion an audience feels for the character are all valid areas for adjudication. Projection may refer to both speech and movement in that both must be large enough to reach the audience. Diction, or clarity of speech, is equally important. Projection and diction constitute the most basic elements of the actor's task—speaking loudly enough to be heard and understood. Gestures should be appropriate to characterization and executed in a smooth and comfortable manner. And movement, too, should be natural and support the telling of the story.

**Endeavor**

In the British model, endeavor addresses the general impact or impression the play made on the audience, the type of play performed, the level of challenge, dramatic merit, suitability for the cast, and the overall concept. These areas of critique are important for the indirect impact they can and arguably should have on adjudication. In the United States, adjudicator guidelines sometimes overlook or ignore these components of the production, but lingering questions remain concerning the balance between the caliber of the dramatic literature involved and quality of the production. If, for example, a very well-done production of *Death of a Salesman* is outperformed by an excellent production of a less demanding play, which play should come out ahead in a ranked adjudication? There are no easy answers. In many states, high school scoring systems do not directly acknowledge degree of difficulty or quality of literature. As a result, directors struggle with play selection. Should they raise the bar for their students by selecting a more challenging piece, or play it safe by selecting a play of lesser value, but greater ease in production?

Nor do easy answers exist in competitive settings where a comedy is up against a dramatic selection and a musical. This "apples and oranges" conversation has continued for more than twenty years with occasional crescendos and decrescendos. The most frustrating part of the director's experience is not the mixed bag of productions at the contest, but the realization that one of your judges "hates" (or "loves") musicals. I have worked alongside too many adjudicators who will score a badly done musical higher than a well-done play simply because they believed the musical was harder to produce, or who will place a musical last in the rankings simply because it was a musical. One reaction is as inappropriate as the other and both reflect the adjudicator's biases rather than legitimate perceptions of what is "good theatre." Furthermore, they are often inconsistent with the rules of adjudication for the festival in question.

Type of play, level of challenge, and dramatic merit come together to answer a basic question: was the selected play worthy of the time and effort given to the production? The adjudicator should address these questions honestly and respectfully by acknowledging appropriate challenges, encouraging the company to reach farther when the level of challenge is too small for the ability of the group, and recognizing a noble effort when the company fails or falters in attaining its goals.

Suitability for the cast also invites comment on the degree of difficulty of a selected title, but has other implications as well. Is the play suitable in terms of the acting abilities of the company? Is the staging appropriate? Is the language and structure of the play acceptable for the cast? Is the content appropriate to the age level of the performers and the audience? I remember one incident where I adjudicated a performance of an absurdist piece. Midway through the play, a young lady in a dress collapses on the floor at the upstage end of a sofa located stage left with her feet extended in a down stage right direction. A few minutes later, the girl began to writhe on stage. The moment was obviously humorous in its intent (and, I would add, had no sexual overtones) but the experience made me, and other members of the audience, so uncomfortable that as an adjudicator I was obligated to address it in my written critique of the play. Fortunately, we were not asked to give an oral critique, saving adjudicator, director and actress the embarrassment of a public conversation about unintended public exposure.

General impact or impression, and overall concept round out the endeavor section of the critique. These elements address the impact the play had on its audience in general, and on the adjudicator in particular. They provide the adjudicator the chance to express that "wow" moment when he got lost in the theatrical experience. These areas free the adjudicator to express pure opinion rather than to share observations from an informed perspective.

These less tangible elements of production decisions warrant consideration in the adjudication process. It is important to talk about the general attainment of a production company. The company set out to accomplish certain goals, and to at least some minimal degree of success, accomplished these goals by participating in the festival. This notion of attainment provides the adjudicator the opportunity to discuss the level of the goals themselves, and the level of success the company reached in attempting them.

A thorough adjudication addresses every element of a theatrical production, dealing with stage presentation, production, directing, ensemble, acting, and endeavor. Each element includes a number of subcategories, covering nearly every aspect of production. The adjudicator is called upon to use these guidelines to assess objectively, comment critically and constructively, and inform the production company and the audience. A summary of the production elements addressed in adjudication appears in the following table.

| Adjudication Production Elements | | | |
|---|---|---|---|
| **Stage Presentation** | **Production** | **Acting** | **Endeavor (Concept)** |
| Setting | Spirit/meaning of the play | Characterization | General impact/ impression |
| Costumes | Team work | Projection | Type of play |
| Props | Pace | Diction | Level of challenge |
| Lighting | Tempo | Expression | Dramatic merit |
| Sound Effects | Stage pictures | Gesture | Suitability for cast |
| Music | The telling of the story | Movement | Overall concept |

In the next chapter, we examine one of the most difficult issues for organizers of adjudicated theatre events: the subject of scoring.

# CHAPTER FIVE

## Choosing a Winner—Scores and Ballots

What must be understood at the outset of any discussion of scoring or marking systems is that one cannot score a work of art. There is no adequate scoring system to measure the work of an actor, the quality of a design concept or its execution. It is impractical to evaluate the work of a costumer by assessing the number of dropped stitches or uneven hems and then converting that observation to a numerical value for the purpose of computation, yet the demands of many festivals and all competitions require that adjudicators do so.

I would also point out that by far my preference is to adjudicate a play without any obligation of assigning a numerical score or festival ranking. This approach allows the adjudicator to focus on the talents and efforts of the performing company and its production team without the adverse, punitive effect of deducting points from a total possible score. The dilemma of point values is especially problematic for those of us in the educational setting where students tend to equate a numerical score with a letter grade. Consistent with that very notion, many scoring systems, including the British model, reflect a one-hundred-point scale. Students of theatre, then, often see a score of 70 or below as "failing the test." Whenever possible, organizers of festivals and competitions should avoid a marking or scoring system that uses numerical values.

## Why Then Do We Use Them?

There are valid reasons why organizers choose to use scoring systems—two external concerns, and one internal concern.

Externally, competition organizers need to know who wins. A scoring system with numerical values is a quick and easily accessible summation of the outcome of a theatre competition. Anyone can look at the scores, whether they agree or disagree with the judges' decisions, and can walk away from the event with a clear understanding of who won and why they won. Organizers of festivals attempt to implement their chosen format as a distinctly different entity from a competition, and do so specifically to avoid this "highest score" mentality, yet the same concerns exist in the festival setting, even if they are somewhat more subtle. If an independent scoring system completed by each adjudicator is not used as part of the process, then the adjudicators are left to determine the outcome through discussion. The result of the adjudication becomes a negotiated settlement, dependent at least in part upon the political leanings of the adjudicators—and which among them are able to mount the most effective argument. Even in the festival setting, some sort of scoring system helps to maintain the integrity of the adjudication.

A second external pressure that promotes the use of a scoring system is the perception of the participating companies. The argument is very similar in nature to the one reflected in the section above, but it is aimed to a different audience. The festival organizers need a clear statement of who won and why so that the participants in the festival, and the audiences attending, can comprehend how a given decision came about. As much as the philosophers and scholars in the industry believe that art should transcend the mundane qualities of a scoring system, we live in a world that understands scores, and in a society that celebrates those who strive to win.

The internal reason for supporting the use of numerical scores speaks to James Dodding's explanation of the true value for any scoring or marking system. In his training sessions, he would tell students "the primary function of any scoring system is to discipline the thinking of the adjudicator." The adjudicator uses the system provided by the festival organizers, or his own system if appropriate, to guide his evaluation of the production aspects evaluated and the weight given to each of those areas. To illustrate this point, we'll consider in detail the criteria set up by high school play competitions in two states, not atypical of the rest of the country, which allot points for different aspects of the production as guidelines to the adjudicator.

## Georgia

The following headings or objectives, with point values assigned to each one, are taken from the Georgia High School Association's (GHSA) official One Act Play Judge's Evaluation Sheet. These major headings on the GHSA scoring system represent the eight areas of production that the festival organizers expect adjudicators to use in their evaluation of the competing company performances.

| | |
|---|---|
| Ensemble | (1–15 points) |
| Listening and Response | (1–15 points) |
| Individual Characterizations | (1–15 points) |

Vocal Interpretation                          (1–15 points)

Movement                                          (1–15 points)

Overall Effect                                      (1–10 points)

Composition and Picturization   (1–10 points)

Rhythm and Tempo                         (1–5 points)

The evaluation form expands on each of these areas by posing a set of basic questions under each category—a sort of prompt to move the adjudicator's mindset into the frame of reference intended for that part of the evaluation. The point distribution appears to start out evenly. The first five objectives constitute 75% of the total possible points. Then the point values change, and the next two assessment objectives drop in value from a maximum of fifteen points to ten points, and the final objective allows a maximum score of only five points. While this change may seem arbitrary, it begins to make sense when one examines more closely the topics addressed.

The first five areas of the score sheet, at first, may seem to reflect what could be considered the more objective areas of production, but there is more to it than that. These topics are weighted more heavily in the scoring because of the rules of the competition, which remind participants and adjudicators alike that the event is an *acting* competition. These first five headings—ensemble, listening and response, individual characterization, vocal interpretation, and use of movement—are all direct elements of the actor's task. These areas reflect the actors' choices as much or more than the director's, and it is the actors' execution that will be evaluated by the adjudicators in order to score this section. If adjudicators implement the rules of the competition, and apply the scoring system as intended, fully 75% of a production's score derives from the work of the actor in this "acting competition."

As the first five areas for evaluation on the GHSA scoring system may appear at first to be more objective, the last three areas—overall impact, composition and picturization, and rhythm and tempo—may appear to be more subjective. Isn't "overall impact" largely an opinion? Are stage pictures and composition not a matter of taste or preference? Can an adjudicator adequately assess the tempo of a selection as effectively and clearly as he can evaluate the use of movement? These areas are less tangible, to be sure, but adjudicators should address them with the same level of objectivity as reflected in the initial five areas of evaluation. The difference, again, is the extent to which these areas focus on and are impacted by, the acting in the production. These last three evaluation areas have lower maximum scores because they do not directly address acting. Overall impact is largely influenced by the perspective and the opinions of the adjudicator. It is the one area of assessment where the adjudicator can validly include his more subjective thoughts. Composition and picturization are determined by the director through blocking, and the rhythm and tempo of a selection are under his control as well. These areas only constitute 25% of the overall possible score. In summary, what may at first appear to be arbitrary or unfounded decisions about the point distribution on the Georgia High School Association One Act Play Evaluation form, is in fact a faithful reflection of the intended nature and stated rules of the contest. Acting constitutes 75% of the total score because acting is the major focus of the event. Directing decisions, and the adjudicators' overall reaction, are less important in the scoring because they are less important in the rules. The same relationship between rules and scoring systems, one would hope, would be true in all festivals and competitions.

## Texas

The Texas Educational Theatre Association (TETA) may have the most comprehensive approach to one act play adjudication. The state's University Interscholastic League (UIL), founded in 1927, sets strict, detailed guidelines for everything from play selection to hosting a competition to establishing a prescribed list of "unit set" pieces that are allowed in participating productions. The UIL publishes an annual *Handbook for One-Act Play*. The nearly 200-page handbook includes a twenty-page guide for judges that articulates the role of the "Critic Judge" as being primarily "to serve as an educator." The chapter on adjudication was developed by the Texas Educational Theatre Association Adjudicators' Organization (TETAAO), founded by TETA in 1988. The judges' guide addresses the function and qualifications, pre-contest judging procedures, working conditions, a glossary of terms, guidelines for awards selection, critique instructions, and criteria for nominating and selecting judges at the area/region and state competitions. The document also includes an operating code and by-laws for TETAAO. The organization's "Standards of Adjudication and Judging Practices" breaks the adjudicator's assessment into two major areas: "acting," valued at "about 60%," and "directing and stage mechanics," worth "about 40%."

## ACTING

The content of the acting portion of the adjudication guidelines include seven areas: voice, characterization, movement, contrast, ensemble, timing, and motivation. Each of these headings includes various elements, specific questions that the critic judge should consider to build an effective critique.

**Voice**: In addition to the basics of voice such as clarity, rate, pronunciation, and audibility, the Texas guidelines include some unusual elements such as attention to the use of closing consonant sounds, and the use of dialect—does it help or hinder with understanding? They also assess the effectiveness of the performers in using inflection and tone to effectively drive the dramatic action.

**Characterization**: Texas adjudicators are asked to address all observations concerning characterization within the "given casting of the actors." Adjudicators address such individual areas of concern as physical and vocal choices that "fully create characters," and a determination of whether actors appear to experience the emotions of their characters, but they are not to question the casting decisions of the director, or the appropriateness of an actor for a given role.

**Movement**: Adjudicators are asked to address movement in context of the actors' characterizations, and in the context of effective control. Pantomime, when used, should be accurate and convincing, and all movement should be intentional.

**Contrast**: In this section of the response, judges assess the use of variety in voices, posture, movement, timing, and other dramatic elements of the performance. Actors are assessed on their effectiveness in creating supported, natural and effective emotional transitions.

**Ensemble**: In the ensemble section of the response, adjudicators address the overall cohesiveness of the action of the play, and the evidence of effective rehearsal and close cooperation among the cast. The adjudicators speak to how tightly knit the show is, and how effectively the rhythm of the piece is played.

**Timing**: Adjudicators use the timing portion of the response to comment on the pace and rate of the performance. They also address the appropriateness of pace to the telling of the story being told.

**Motivation**: Are the movements, stage business and actions of the actors consistent with the given circumstances and characters of the play? Adjudicators respond to this question, and assess the suggestion of intuitiveness in the actors' work.

## DIRECTING AND STAGE MECHANICS

The section on directing and stage mechanics also covers seven areas of production. The areas of concern include:

- Blocking, Composition, Picturization, Stage Business
- Tempo and Mood
- Theme/Style
- Ground Plan and Set Design
- Costume and Make-up
- Lighting
- Sound Effects and Music

In each of these areas, as in the acting portion of the response, the guidelines provide a series of detailed questions to assist the adjudicator in the response.

These adjudication and judging practices as they appear in the *Handbook for One-Act Play* do not represent a form or document to be used in the adjudication process. In fact, the document is structured using yes or no questions akin to a check list. This approach, in the context of an actual form that must be completed, would tend to limit the ability of the adjudicators to make positive, constructive comments to students about their work. Nonetheless, the Texas guidelines are thorough and help the critic judge to address numerous areas of production.

In contrast to TETA's critic judges, the Georgia Thespian organization uses "screeners" to make recommendations for productions that should be invited to perform at state conference and international conferences.

## International Thespians

The International Thespian Society does not promote theatrical competition, but throughout their network, high school theatre programs are given the opportunity to bring their productions to perform at annual regional, state, and even international conferences. To facilitate this process, the organization engages in a screening process, not to name "winners," but to determine which productions from across the state or across the country are invited to perform. In most circumstances, a committee of at least three "screeners" must see a production interested in performing at conference, and at least two of those screeners must agree that the production should be invited. In assessing a production, screeners evaluate a total of thirteen elements: Selection; Interpretation; Tempo & Rhythm; Blocking, Composition & Picturization; Characterization; Ensemble; Dance; Technical; Lighting; Set; Costumes & Makeup; Sound & Music; and the Overall Effect of the Production. Scoring, except for the assessment of the selection itself, is based on a scale of superior, excellent, good and fair. In each of these areas of assessment, screeners are provided space to make comments about the production.

The discussion herein is based on the Colorado State Thespian Screening Committee Form, but forms in other states, and those used for screening invitations to the international conference held each June in Lincoln, Nebraska, are very similar in form and content.

## Selection
- Was the script within the emotional capabilities of the cast?
- Does this script have either strong entertainment and/or educational value?
- Does the selection highlight the troupe's talents?

## Interpretation
- Is the director's interpretation consistent and well thought through?
- Does the director's concept capture the playwright's intent?
- Did the cast understand the director's concept?
- Musical—Are the singers interpreting the songs (as opposed to merely singing the notes)?

## Tempo, Rhythm

- Did the play move smoothly?
- Did the tempo/pace assist the mood of the play?
- Was the tempo/rhythm in keeping with the playwright's intent?
- Did the actors pick up lines/cues?
- Were the non-speaking moments effective in the tempo/rhythm of the delivery of the play?
- Was there good energy?

## Blocking, Composition, Picturization

- Was the blocking interesting?
- Was the stage used effectively?
- Were attractive pictures created on stage?
- Were different levels used?
- Was the blocking natural and comfortable?

## Characterization

- Were the characters believable?
- Was there depth in the development of each character?
- Were the characters consistent?
- Were the actors committed to their characters?
- Were relationships established between the characters?
- Were the actors playing objectives rather than emotions?

## Ensemble

- Did the ensemble exhibit teamwork and interaction?
- Was the ensemble able to avoid any "star" personalities?
- Was the ensemble used to its full potential?

## Dance
- Was the choreography interesting to watch?
- Was the choreography within the capabilities of the cast?

## Technical
- Do the technical aspects of this production work to support the director's concept?
- Do all the technical aspects of the production work together?

## Lighting
- Did the lighting enhance the overall appearance of the production?
- Were the performance areas well defined by lighting?
- Were inappropriate shadows or poorly lit areas avoided?
- Were the lighting cues on time?
- Were the gobos used with valid purpose?
- Musical—Did the lighting change to support the builds in the music and tempo changes?

## Set
- Was the scenery attractive and engaging to look at?
- Were the set pieces relevant to the story?
- Was attention paid to a design concept?
- Did the set design support the period of the play?
- Did the set work for the delivery of the text?
- Was the set well built and safe?

## Costumes/Makeup
- Did the costumes support the concept and period of the play?

- Were the costumes consistent in their design for the entire cast?
- Were the costumes well made?
- Did the makeup support the age and personality of the characters?
- Was the makeup applied skillfully?

## Sound, Music
- Did the sound/music support the mood of the play?
- Could each character be heard?
- Were the sound cues on time?
- Musical—Did the musicians perform the songs well?

## Overall Effect of the Production
- Did all the aspects of the production, technical and performance, work together to present a cohesive show?

At the end of the Thespian screening committee form, adjudicators are given additional space for any final comments. Screeners make their actual invitation recommendation on a separate form that is not shared with the director.


## Kennedy Center/American College Theatre Festival

The Kennedy Center/American College Theatre Festival program provides a means for college and university theatre directors to submit their work for peer review. College programs that choose to take part in the program submit productions as either associate or participating productions.

While some states still require productions to travel to a state festival to take part in the process, most theatre programs host the respondent(s) in their local venue. One respondent attends a performance when a production participates as an associate entry. Two respondents attend a participating entry's performance. In each case, the respondents have the same responsibilities: 1) to provide an oral response in a "talk back" format following the performance; and 2) to submit, electronically, a written response to the production—ideally within 72 hours of seeing the performance. A region chairperson reviews the response and forwards it to the director.

Aside from the number of respondents, the other major distinction between associate and participating entries in the festival is that, in normal circumstances, only participating entries are eligible for an invitation to advance to the regional festival. At the regional event, respondents select productions that will be invited to move on to the national festival in Washington, D.C. KC/ACTF organizes the United States into eight regions, and the total number of theatre entries can vary greatly from year to year and from region to region. As many as 200 entries might register in a given year. Of that number, 60-80 productions are typically participating rather than associate entries. While a committee of respondents selects as many as five or six plays to invite to the regional festival, former Region IV Chair Jeff Gibson pointed out that the focus is not on filling a quota or ensuring that a minimum number of plays perform. He explained that the goal of the process was to select the very best productions from across the region to come and share their work with others.

Like other festival formats, the KC/ACTF process does provide opportunities for outstanding productions to move to the next level, but is not a competitive event. Organizers are emphatic about the distinction between competition and festival. The respondent in the KC/ACTF model is not making judgments about a production. He is not an adjudicator, and the language of adjudication is strongly discouraged.

Guidelines provided by the organization remind respondents that "responding is respectful of the work and the process..." and that the response is "one person's response, not a definitive word," and usually open their oral response with some sort of statement to this effect. KC/ACTF respondents must address five areas of the production: choice of play; direction; acting; design elements; and technical elements.

### Choice of Play
Respondents discuss their perception of the appropriateness of the play for a college/university production. They reflect on whether the selection is a good choice to be advanced in the festival. In this context, they establish for the listeners their criteria for making such a recommendation, and share their views on how and to what extent the production team met the standard.

### Direction
In the directing portion of the response, respondents define the director's concept as they understood it, and reflect on the viability of the concept for the play. Was the concept successful and consistently realized? Was the casting consistent with the concept? How did it appear that the director worked with the cast? Did the director illustrate adequate control of the production? Were stage pictures balanced and effective? Was movement clearly defined and executed?

## Acting

In productions with smaller casts, the respondent addresses the work of each performer individually. In larger-cast productions, the response may include a discussion of the ensemble, perhaps highlighting certain individual performers. The respondent may reflect on technical ability of the actors, interpretation of character, ensemble performance, movement, period, dialect, and various other elements of the actors' work.

## Design Elements

KC/ACTF trainers note that even respondents who do not have a design background should address the design elements of the production in their response. Respondents are encouraged to speak about how the design elements contributed to the production. They can look for artistic excellence, and reflect on how the design elements functioned within the context of the play. They should also explore the connection between the design elements, the director's concept, and the actors' choices.

## Technical Elements

The final area on which the respondent should focus involves the various technical elements of the production. In this section of the presentation, the respondent should address the execution of the design elements of the production. How well were they executed? How well did the show run? What improvements in technical elements might help the production?

The KC/ACTF guidelines even go so far as to suggest structures or approaches that a respondent might use to frame the presentation of oral and written comments. One such framework is the problem-solving method, in which the commentator poses questions about the problems and traps in a given production, and then leads a discussion with the company in which they seek and evaluate various solutions. From this beginning, the respondent can address a number of challenges about the play selection, the theatre space, the choices made by actors, designers and directors, the risks they chose to take, and so on.

In contrast to the problem-solving method, a respondent may choose to use a purely chronological approach in which he reflects on his journey through the theatre experience in the sequence in which the journey took place. This framework for response provides opportunities to cite specific quotes and discuss particularly moving moments from the beginning to the end of the play. Some respondents actually incorporate their entrance into the theatre lobby, dramaturgical or other lobby displays, and even the post-show experience. This approach to responding to a production appears to be often used and generally well received.

KC/ACTF training materials suggest, "Respondents can say almost anything about a play if they are connected with and not isolated from the company; they are perceived as truthful, sensitive, and knowledgeable; and they organize effectively the information they wish to present." Trainers emphasize the importance of covering all areas of the production—choice of play, directing, acting, design and technical—in both oral and written commentary. They also warn that the written response should reinforce the oral critique rather than disagree with it or go in a different direction. The written response should never be used to bring up issues or criticisms that the respondent did not want to address in person, though it can be used to elaborate on critical concerns (and commendations) shared in the oral response.

The KC/ACTF approach is perhaps best summarized in the notion that the "language of adjudication is strongly discouraged." Their philosophy is clear and articulate in making the distinction between a festival and a competitive setting. While outstanding productions are invited to showcase in regional and national festivals, the focus of the Kennedy Center response is on the learning. The primary distinction between the language of the respondent and the language of the adjudicator involves the making of judgments. Adjudicators do it. Respondents do not.

As part of my research in writing this text, I went through the training process to become a KC/ACTF adjudicator. I came away from the training experience with the understanding that an adjudicator comes into a production as a sort of expert. He observes and assesses the performance, makes judgments about the effectiveness of the decisions made by the production team, the cast, and the technical crews, and then articulates, orally and in written form, his defense for the conclusions he made. The respondent, on the other hand, comes to the theatre to experience the production. His presentations, both oral and written, constitute a sharing of that experience.

The distinction between adjudicator and respondent seems to be clear-cut at first glance, but all too often, the difference is lost in the delivery of an oral response. Even the most experienced respondents can occasionally slide into subtle value judgments without realizing it. In a scenario where an adjudicator might say that a given moment did not work, the respondent might ask the actors or director in the scene what they were working to accomplish, and then explain the reaction he had to the moment and how his reaction related to their goals. On the surface, then, the difference between adjudicator and respondent is more than simply scores and rankings. The goals and motivations themselves are subtly different.

## The American Association of Community Theatres

In 1971, the American Community Theatre Association, the predecessor to the current American Association of Community Theatres (AACT) hosted its first national festival with actor Henry Fonda, New York drama critic William Glover, and Guthrie Theatre artistic director Michael Langham serving as adjudicators. Since then, the National Festival (AACTFest) has been hosted in odd-numbered years by community theatres across the country. The national festival came as a result of the United States' first entry in the World Festival of Amateur Theatre in 1965, and the realization that the country needed a viable process to select a high-quality production to represent the U.S. in the international setting. Over the nearly forty years since the inception of the national festival, AACT has developed and refined the guidelines for adjudication of festival productions. According to the 2011 AACTFest handbook, adjudication should be based on overall pro-duction with acting and directing as the major elements. Adjudicators are to accept all production types and genres, evaluating each on similar criteria, and the best production should be "the one most fully realizing all production values and criteria." Adjudicators are not to question play selection, though they may address the appropriateness of the selection for the company. Otherwise, they may speak only to how the play was performed. AACT provides a series of questions to be considered by the adjudicators:

- Is the acting believable and technically skillful with effective timing?

- Are the characters well interpreted?
- Does the company display ensemble work?
- Is the material appropriate for the company?
- Is the concept appropriate for the material and realized by the company?
- Has the structure of the production been controlled?
- Are the movements and stage pictures effective?
- Is the production well paced?
- Do the technical elements support the overall production?
- How effective was the total impact?

Adjudicators are encouraged to focus on positive solutions, and encouraged to offer alternate choices, but are sternly warned that it is not their role to redirect the show. The adjudicators are not to be concerned with rules violations. They are to attend to the performances themselves, and allow festival organizers to address concerns about the rules.

In AACT, a Festival Commission Representative or Festival Commission Chair designee is charged with providing an orientation session for adjudicators and other relevant personnel. In the session, they review the AACT Adjudicator Responsibilities and Guidelines, the timing regulations, the time allotted and the sequence for oral adjudications following each performance. A panel discussion format may be used at state and region festivals, at the discretion of the organizers for each individual festival, but the panel approach may not be used at the national festival.

The orientation also includes a review of the awards to be considered, and information about the official balloting process. Adjudicators are informed that they will be subject to formal evaluation by observers who meet criteria defined by AACT, and that they will eventually receive a report of that evaluation. They are also informed that they may sit in any seat in the house, but they must sit in the same seat for all performances, and that they will be expected to use a microphone for the oral commentary.

AACT provides strict guidelines concerning the interaction between adjudicators during the festival experience. Adjudicators are monitored throughout the process, including during breaks and meals, to ensure that there is no discussion about the productions they see. While each adjudicator delivers an oral critique, fellow adjudicators are removed to a location where they cannot hear the commentary. This approach to handling adjudicators marks an effort to avoid undue influence by one adjudicator on the outcome of the festival.

The AACT process does not require the adjudicator to provide a written adjudication. The organization does not provide a specific form or format for written comments. They expect adjudicators to provide a thorough oral critique and complete a balloting process to select the winning production.

## The Ethics of Adjudication: Raw Scores vs. Rankings

The moral and ethical obligation of any adjudicator is to adhere faithfully to the scoring system provided by the festival or contest sponsors, and to execute his responsibilities in a professional and consistent manner. In reality, though, there are unscrupulous adjudicators in the field who do not adhere to this philosophy. Some are subtle and relatively innocent in the error of their ways. Others are more direct—even blatant—in their disrespect for the guidelines provided by the festival sponsors who invite them to serve, pay their expenses, and provide them with a stipend or honorarium.

The most egregious offense I have witnessed in my quarter century of adjudication came early in my career when I participated in evaluating a community theatre festival. There were only three of four productions in the event, but adjudicators were required to declare a winner that would move forward to the next level of competition. Adjudicators were provided with rules of the contest and appropriate scoring sheets reflecting a 100-point scale. Three judges made independent assessments and turned their completed score sheets in to the contest coordinator who would add the total points assigned for each play to determine the winner. Two of the judges involved, myself included, adhered to the philosophy stated earlier in this section— that is to adhere faithfully to the scoring system and execute his responsibilities in a professional and consistent manner. The third adjudicator, though, did something I am thankful to say I have only seen once in my career. While commenting to us aloud that he knew which show should win, and intended to make certain it did, he scored his choice for best play at 100 points, and then assigned a score of less than ten points to each of the other plays in the contest. With the stroke of a pen he assured it was mathematically impossible for any other play to win, completely nullifying any possible impact the other judges may have had on the outcome. The fact that all three adjudicators agreed on which production was strongest does not diminish the appalling behavior of the offending adjudicator.

This horrifying experience was exceptional in its audacity, but it provided the basis for an understanding that there are too many uncontrolled variables in a 100-point scoring system. The offending adjudicator, of course, was never invited back, and in one sense no harm was done since the other two adjudicators were in agreement with the final outcome. Still, the incident magnified the potential for problems to develop that could compromise the integrity of the adjudication. Ultimately, because of this kind of incident, both the Georgia Theatre Conference and the Georgia High School Association moved to one-act play scoring systems that used rankings rather than raw scores to determine the outcome of festivals and competitions. The process for the adjudicators was the same. Adjudicators scored plays on a 100-point scale, and ranked each play (1st place, 2nd place, etc.) according to the scores. The festival host then added the rankings for each play, and the low score won the event. A play, for example, that received three first-place rankings had a tallied score of three and was unbeatable. The system still allowed for manipulation on the part of an unscrupulous judge, especially in larger festivals, but the new approach to scoring severely limited any chance that a single adjudicator could swing the outcome of scoring irrespective of the other judges participating in the evaluation. Only in the case of a tie were raw scores used to determine the outcome of an event.

**Avoiding the Appearance of Impropriety**

In Dr. Pangloss' best of all possible worlds, festival organizers would not find the need to implement strategies to protect the integrity of the evaluation process, but the reality is that there exist judges who—consciously or unconsciously—allow bias, politics, and other distractions to influence their perceptions of plays. In order to prevent or eliminate such problems, our "profession" must be more willing to police itself, and individual adjudicators as well as festival organizers must make and adhere to a firm commitment to avoid even the appearance of impropriety. In recent one-act play seasons, I can share three experiences that clearly allowed for the appearance of impropriety.

My first illustration involves a festival I hosted. The Georgia High School Association, as noted earlier, establishes classifications based on student population and then divides each classification into regions. We hosted a region competition on our campus at Camden County High School. As an administrator, I am not involved in directing the competition play, but our school was one of the participants. I asked a director from a neighboring community to adjudicate for us, and she agreed. She used to compete against us but her school dropped to a lower classification a few years ago. A week before the scheduled contest, I participated in a competition where, as it turned out, my friend was competing. When I learned of the potential conflict of interest I approached my friend, talked through the situation, and respectfully withdrew the invitation. She was supportive of my position, and understood the appearance of impropriety. I found a substitute adjudicator at the beginning of the following week.

The region winner in our GHSA one-act play competition goes on to participate in the State Championship. One year the state festival organizers called upon one of the adjudicators who judged our region competition to cover a last-minute cancellation at the state contest. The adjudicator agreed without realizing or giving thought to the classification she was being asked to judge. As fate would have it, one of the state judges had judged our play at the region level just one week before the state championship festival. This situation, too, appeared to lend itself to misinterpretation and may have made other contestants who were aware of the incident uncomfortable, regardless of whether it might be an advantage or a disadvantage to the production scored twice by the same adjudicator.

In yet another true story illustrating the appearance of impropriety, I judged a contest where one of the other judges and I had the same rankings on three of the top four productions. The third judge disagreed, placing our choice for best play second to another production. I later learned, quite by accident, that the following day the adjudicator that assigned the first place ranking to a different play participated in his own region contest, adjudicated by the director of the play that he placed first the day before. The potential for the appearance of impropriety is blatantly obvious in this example.

I should note here that in most competitive settings the adjudicators do not receive information concerning which productions come from which schools, yet in many set-tings, they know anyway. State and local play competitions do not usually have the budget to bring in out-of-state evaluators any more than the local football game can afford to bring in out-of-state referees. As colleagues in the rela-tively small network of play producers and directors, we adjudicators easily become familiar with one another's work. This awareness in and of itself is not improper. Still, festival organizers should take note, and avoid awkward situations concerning the relationship between adjudicator and participant whenever possible.

When concerns about the integrity of a contest become a topic of conversation, when festival evaluation arrange-ments suggest the appearance of impropriety, everyone loses regardless of the accuracy of the perception. If adju-dication is going to develop as a profession, then individual adjudicators and festival and contest organizers must work together to exemplify high standards of evaluation that remove any suggestion of compromise based on personal relationships between adjudicators and directors of the politics of the sponsoring organization. Such an approach can only enhance the reputation of the field of adjudication.

## Which Is the "Correct" Procedure?

When evaluating a theatrical performance in a festival or contest, the adjudicator can most certainly find as many scoring systems as there are sponsoring organizations. No one process or set of guidelines is the "correct" procedure. All are acceptable because each is appropriate to the goals and interests of the organization that created it. The task for the adjudicator is to apply the guidelines provided by the festival sponsors in a consistent and ethical manner. Ideally, the adjudicator should try to address every area of a production as described at the beginning of this chapter, but addressing these areas and acknowledging the work of various members of the production does not give license for the adjudicator to incorporate all of them into the scoring. Actual scoring should adhere closely and strictly to the guidelines or rules provided.

Festival or contest organizers should work closely with the adjudicators to avoid any appearance of impropriety that could prompt participants or patrons of the event to call into question the integrity of the outcome. Personal relationships and organizational politics cannot and should not play a part in adjudication. In the practical world, the existence of personal relationships between directors and evaluators cannot always be avoided and do not automatically negate the integrity of the festival nor the validity of the outcome, but all interested parties should work together and use sound judgment as to when certain arrangements should be avoided. An adjudicator interested in maintaining a professional demeanor should take extra care to avoid any suggestion that personal relationships or biases influenced his evaluation. Any adjudicator who would do otherwise is not worthy of respect.

The content of adjudication and the scoring of a play are still only part of the responsibilities of an adjudicator. In the next chapter, we will discuss the final element of the process—the shape and delivery of a formal adjudication.

# CHAPTER SIX

## The Shape of a Formal Adjudication

The final element of an adjudicator's work is the delivery
of the formal adjudication to the production team or audience gathered to hear the response. As with scoring, I do
not offer the "correct" approach, or even the "definitive"
approach. I do offer guidelines, promoted by my mentor
James Dodding, that, compared to many practices around
the country, may seem stuffy and a little formal, but have
clear merits as a strategy to move adjudication towards
professional status. Whether you use the Dodding method,
or your adjudication takes the shape developed by the
Kennedy Center/American College Theatre Festival or the
American Community Theatre Association, I think you'll
find these suggestions equally applicable.

### A Formal Presentation

Not every festival or contest requests, expects or allows an
oral critique, but many do have such an expectation.
Dodding firmly believed an adjudicator's oral remarks
should be consistent in shape and format—both within the
evaluation of a specific play and throughout the festival,
from production to production, so that the audience could
acclimate to the approach and style of each evaluator and
follow a clear, sequenced comparison of remarks, though
not of productions. In other words, the purpose of the
evaluation, whether written or oral, is not to compare one
production to another, but to compare each production to its

own potential. The production team and the audience should be able to follow the adjudicator through the critique in a manner that enables them to comprehend and process the observations, then draw their own conclusions concerning the quality of the performance. In this regard, he recommended a specific strategy that I still use today in my own adjudication, and in training sessions. Effective critiques are formal in delivery, consistent in structure, constructive in content, uplifting in style, and ultimately educational in nature.

## Formal Delivery

The adjudicator should deliver his critique in a formal manner, maintaining ideally a physical and at least an aesthetic distance between himself and the production team and listening audience. He should project adequately to reach the entire audience. His speech should demonstrate crisp, clear diction, easily understood. He should choose words more formal than casual; street speech is not acceptable. He should speak from the perspective of first person, singular when in reference to his individual observations or reactions, plural when in reference to the audience perspective. He should direct his comments to the company in the third person rather than second. Some of these choices may seem at first to be stuffy and distant, but consider the impact on a production company as reflected in the story illustrated in the introduction.

As reported, an adjudicator walked directly up to the young actress playing Antigone, peered over his half-lenses, and declared "you were not interesting." Would the incident have carried the same weight with the performer or the company if he had been standing a safe distance away from the company, and said, "The young actress playing Antigone failed to capture my interest"? Would the performer have perceived the comment to be as hurtful as it was in the way the adjudicator actually delivered it? I think not. The aesthetic distance between evaluator and performer, combined with the third person structure of the commentary, delivered the same content with less emotional distress. This illustration is just one of many examples that demonstrate the value of maintaining a formal delivery in oral adjudication.

The adjudicator should intentionally deliver his comments to the audience as a whole. This recommendation is among the most controversial when I share my views with fellow evaluators. Many practicing adjudicators want to focus on establishing a personal rapport with the cast and crew of the production. They speak from the floor of the auditorium, just a few feet away from the actors. They sometimes speak softly and walk up to the individuals to whom they are speaking, completely ignoring a captive and often captivated audience straining to hear the evaluation. This practice is unfair to the patrons of theatre who attended the event and expected to hear the critiques. Theatrical adjudication warrants a formal delivery, presentational in style.

## Consistent Structure

When there is a written commentary or scoring system, an adjudicator's oral remarks should be consistent in structure with it. The adjudicator should respect and not abandon this structure within the delivery of a given critique. He should also maintain a consistent structure, or shape, for the adjudication from one oral critique to the next, just as he does in the application of written comments to a structured score sheet.

I would like to begin with some general remarks about the play and its demands, and then turn to specific observations in each of the first three categories or productions areas reflected in the model: stage presentation; production; and acting, including each of the appropriate subcategories under each of these production elements, and then close with a few words to sum up the total effect of the prouction. These closing remarks would address the final production element, endeavor.

If the adjudicator were to follow the sample cited in the chapter on scoring, he would begin with a general comment similar to that found in the British model, and then address the five acting areas found at the beginning of the GHSA score sheet: Ensemble, Listening and Response; Individual Characterizations, Vocal Interpretation; and Movement. I would recommend at that point that the evaluator stray from the structure of the score sheet by moving to Composition and Picturization, and then Rhythm and Tempo, before addressing the Overall Effect, the latter of which would close the critique.

Whether using one of these examples or another structure based on a different model, the adjudicator should lay out the format for the audience, then be careful to adhere to that format within the critique so that listeners can easily follow the commentary and make sense of the observations shared. The oral critique can often reflect a lack of organization, and occasionally a lack of coherent thought, in the adjudicator. Responses that bounce back and forth between various production elements are much more difficult to follow than those that succeed in categorizing observations and sharing them in a more structured manner.

The adjudicator must also consistently adhere to the structure chosen throughout the entire festival. An audience will very quickly develop an ear for a given evaluator. Listeners discern how an adjudicator approaches and structures his evaluations; and if the evaluator changes the structure of his critique midway through a contest or after each play, the audience may get lost and frustrated trying to follow the commentary. Ideally, while the adjudicator should not be comparing one production to another as part of the oral (or written) critique, the audience should be able to easily follow the structure of each adjudicators critiques and, by lining them up alongside one another, get a sense of the adjudicator's position on the strength of each play in comparison to the others. Consistent structure from one evaluation to the next will help to reach the desired effect.

## Constructive Content

Most readers have at least a basic understanding of the difference between constructive and destructive criticism. This distinction is critical in the work of adjudication. A professional adjudicator is living up neither to expectations nor to his title if he engages in destructive commentary. An effective adjudication should focus on honest observations about the production while remaining constructive in content and demeanor, both in verbal and non-verbal communication.

Constructive commentary begins with word choice and sentence structure, written or spoken. An effective adjudicator can thoughtfully share his observations without resorting to any sort of derogatory language or negative terms. The words he chooses should be more formal than casual; more professional than personal; more suggestive than judgmental. Oftentimes a specific word communicates a specific tone. The adjudicator must be aware of this possibility and act accordingly.

When focusing on constructive commentary, the adjudicator must also keep nonverbal communication choices in mind. At the beginning of my career when I taught at the college level, I used a public speaking text entitled *The Challenge of Effective Speaking* by Rudolph Verderber. In it, the author reported that on average, only 7% of the impact of an effort to communicate comes from word choice. The other 93% of the effectiveness of any effort at communication comes from nonverbal communication. Nonverbal communication comes in two forms: vocal and non-vocal.

Nonverbal, vocal communication refers to the variables, or "adjustable settings" of the voice. These qualities include pitch, rate, breath support, rhythm, general tone of voice, overall inflection, and other qualities that a speaker often manipulates to communicate his message. An effective adjudicator must be conscious of the impact of these nonverbal elements of his speech, and use them to communicate and support the intent of his commentary, avoiding inappropriate choices in delivery. Keeping an aesthetic distance as suggested in an earlier chapter, the adjudicator should maintain a professional, perhaps even clinical tone, avoiding any suggestion of condescension. He must also be conscious of vocal pauses—oft-unintended utterances a speaker uses to fill time. Such pauses are sometimes verbal. "Like" and "you know" are two vocal pauses that often occur in speech as "filler" that has no intended meaning pertinent to the message being communicated. Other vocal pauses are non-verbal utterances such as "uh," "um," or "er." In the most common situations where a speaker engages in vocal pause, the utterance reverts to the speaker's base pitch, losing all inflection completely. All speakers should avoid this habit or work to correct it, but the adjudicator in particular needs to be conscious that excessive use of vocal pause communicates a lack of preparation or credibility on the part of the speaker.

Speakers can effectively use silence, or pause, as a means of communicating their message. A silent pause as the adjudicator considers the proper word choice more often than not communicates the notion that the speaker is carefully considering the best way to address a topic. Filling such silence with vocalized sound of any kind tends more to suggest that the speaker is "covering" because he is not sure what to say. Adjudicators who master this challenge of delivery communicate an air of confidence and competence that builds the relationship between themselves and their listening audience, but these vocalizations are still only a part of the nonverbal elements of communication. Adjudicators should also be vigilant in what they communicate through non-vocal means.

Elements of nonverbal, non-vocal communication most often concern body language, but also include facial expression, gesture, and other physical elements that contribute to the communication process without the use of the human voice. Each of these areas can work independently or together to support or contradict the intention of an adjudicator's critique.

Let us return for yet another visit to our adjudicator from the introduction to the text. He approached the young actress playing Antigone, stepping directly up to her to say, "You...were not...interesting!" Consider the body language: he was taller than the student was, and walked up to her until he was close enough to, quite literally, look down at her. He tilted his head, which helped to send a message of condescension. He looked out over his half-lenses, suggesting that he was scolding her and had perhaps lost patience. He abandoned any suggestion of aesthetic distance. His body language was more than just unfriendly; it was intentionally imposing and, at times, even threatening. His facial expression communicated no sense of compassion, understanding or mercy. Gestures were minimal, given that he held a clipboard in one hand and a pencil in the other, but he did manage to raise an accusing finger at her as he made his declaration. His actions, of course, provide a vivid example of how these elements of nonverbal communication can enhance the intended message of the critique; but they also illustrate how damaging an adjudicator can be when he loses sight of his mission or otherwise chooses to be as harsh as possible.

An effective adjudicator must be conscious of his use of body language, facial expression and gesture in delivering a critique. He can implement nonverbal techniques in a variety of constructive ways to clarify, emphasize, indicate nuance, or otherwise enhance the message; but he can also use the same skill set to embarrass, chastise, or even humiliate a production team. To avoid these traps, adjudicators must constantly remind themselves of the mission to which they were called, and which they agreed to try in good faith to fulfill.

## Uplifting Style

No one enjoys a negative adjudicator for any extended length of time. The process of sharing one's work and receiving immediate feedback should be an uplifting experience, and can be so without being dishonest. Up to this point in the text I have offered several examples of how an adjudicator can deliver a challenging message in a way that is constructive rather than destructive. To further this discussion, I offer in this section a brief list of tips that can help to maintain the proper mood of a critique. These suggestions apply primarily to the spoken adjudication, but many can be adapted to written responses as well.

The desire to provide an uplifting experience to those receiving adjudication is yet another reason for the adjudicator to maintain a formal delivery style. The aesthetic distance established by a formal presentation provides a safety zone for the performers. It is no less rewarding for the production team to hear recognition for work well done in a formal setting than in an intimate one. On the contrary, the formal critique is often more rewarding for its positive comments because the observations become public declarations rather than thoughts shared "in private." Negative comments, on the other hand, while equally "public" in a formal critique, diminish in power because the words come from a "distance"—aesthetically, at least. In other words, the words hurt less because when spoken in third person, they cannot make a direct hit on the subject.

I often remind audiences that with the possible exceptions of those who attend auto racing and hockey games, most people who go to a competitive event, want to see the participants succeed. Race fans may go for the crashes; hockey fans for the fights, but everyone else hopes to see competitors perform well. The play competition is no exception. In this regard, the adjudicator should always keep in mind that every team in the contest arrived with the intent and desire to do their very best. They want the best for themselves and their audience. The adjudicator should further remember that the audience in attendance wants the best from each participant in the festival and, for that matter, from each adjudicator. Finally, the adjudicator usually wants to see the best possible productions, and wants to do his best in responding to them.

This notion of wanting the best, often forgotten in adjudication, is a guiding force for the adjudicator. Some respondents pounce on weakness with almost a vengeance. An alternate, more meaningful approach to adjudication that might provide audience and participants with a more rewarding experience might be to report what the production team did best, and what they might do to become even better. What was the best that each production had to offer? What is the best that the adjudicator can say about each performance? And what areas can be improved so that these good things can become better as a result of the adjudication experience? Everyone wants to do their best, to be the best that they can be. By factoring this trait of human nature into the overall response, an adjudicator brings meaning and value to the critique, making it an uplifting experience for all involved.

An adjudicator should never communicate the suggestion that the work of adjudication is burdensome. In context, decisions may be challenging in terms of naming a best play or citing outstanding individual performances, but the work of adjudication itself should never be a burden. Those individuals who find it such should politely decline to adjudicate.

In my own experience, I find an invitation to adjudicate to be an honor. When asked to share my expertise, I become aware of the awesome responsibility that accompanies the task, and I am inspired to move forward with caution and a deep sense of humility. It is a privilege to view the work of others and share my thoughts. One approach I use to promote an uplifting experience for the production team and audience in a festival or contest is a simple, sincere acknowledgment of the effort put forth in the production, and a "thank you" to the company for bringing it to share.

## Educational in Nature

Finally, and ultimately, the shape of any formal adjudication should be educational in nature. An artist who shares his work in a public forum and invites responses from others who are often strangers, does so for one purpose—to become better at what he does. Adjudication is educational in nature. The adjudicator is an educator, and must remember this role at all times. He should not try to prove himself an expert—the invitation for him to serve has already recognized him as one. He should remain always open to new ideas and new learning, demonstrating through example the concept of lifelong learning. He should address every area of production, as every member of the team worked hard and thus warranted some sort of acknowledgment or recognition.

Adjudicators must remember that they are not entertainers. It is neither their goal to demonstrate their wit nor their responsibility to get a laugh. They should treat the performer and the production team as educators, with the respect due the seeking learner. The performer, the production team, and the listening audience should all be better artists, better people, for the experience.

# CHAPTER SEVEN

## Implementing the Concepts: Suggestions for Hosts and Adjudicators

Previous chapters of the text offered discussion, in considerable detail, concerning the background, purpose, content, scoring, and general shape of theatre adjudication. This chapter addresses key steps that festival sponsors or contest organizers might take to implement an effective program of adjudication that will enhance the experience of participants and patrons of theatre events. Topics include suggestions for the selection of adjudicators, provisions to arrange for the adjudicators, recommended guidelines, and the remuneration they can expect for their services.

### Selecting Adjudicators

Festival organizers can most effectively implement and take advantage of the adjudication process if they go into the festival with a plan for selecting adjudicators. Typically, high school associations require three adjudicators for region and state competitions as well as for any competition sanctioned (but not sponsored) by the organization. In Georgia, the association guidelines recommend that whenever possible the contest coordinator recruit two judges affiliated with high school production and one college-level instructor. While one or two judges may be acceptable for festival settings where scoring is not involved and no best play or production award is given, the recommendation of three adjudicators for competitive events is one means to minimize the possibility of unbreakable ties, and promotes credibility in the festival by distributing the responsibility of selecting a winner. Festival organizers can further strengthen their selection of adjudicators by considering experience, references, and affiliations in their efforts to avoid even the appearance of impropriety.

By recommending that festival sponsors should consider the experience of potential adjudicators, I do not suggest that organizers should invite only experienced respondents to adjudicate—every evaluator must start somewhere. In addition to experience in adjudication, coordinators can consider work experience, directing credits, and educational background as part of the experience justifying adjudicator selection. Teaching experience is also a possible indicator of an individual's qualifications to adjudicate. All of these qualities can help to assess the potential of prospective adjudicators.

Organizers of play festivals are encouraged to consider references when selecting adjudicators. This resource is particularly important when considering an unfamiliar adjudicator, an unknown entity. Sponsors might contact references provided by the adjudicators themselves, but might also establish contact with other festival hosts who have used a given adjudicator. The information provided by references can be invaluable in assessing an adjudicator's rapport with production teams and with the audience in general. Conversation with references is a particularly effective means of determining any potential problems or red flags that might not be immediately apparent.

The final element of adjudicator selection that festival organizers are encouraged to consider is affiliation. This factor, more than any single element of adjudicator qualifications, has the greatest potential to create controversy and questions of impropriety in a festival's outcome. Contest organizers should never bring two adjudicators affiliated with the same institution to adjudicate in a festival. Even when the concern is unfounded, it creates the impression of a "stacked deck." I once served on an adjudication panel where a team of directors brought a participating, and ultimately the winning, play. Later that season I served on a panel of judges that included that directing team, and the director of one of the competing plays had judged their production. That director's play won the second event, and while the decision was unanimous, the situation could easily have been misinterpreted. I once hosted a contest where I asked a married couple to serve as two of the three adjudicators. Again, the result was a unanimous decision, and I know firsthand that the operation maintained appropriate ethical standards, but it was the last time I asked a couple to participate in adjudication. Like the first example, this one allowed for the appearance of impropriety.

Affiliations are a factor not just with institutions, but with individuals as well. Ideally, adjudicators would not know the directors of festival productions at all, but in the relatively small world of educational theatre, this ideal is often unreachable. Still, whenever possible, the adjudicators should have limited knowledge or connections with directors competing in an event.

These suggestions concerning the selection of adjudicators are not meant to imply that adjudicators cannot be trusted. In many of the situations cited here, the adjudicators proved to be above reproach—but the selection of adjudicators affects more than just the outcome of the event. It also affects the perceptions of the patrons, the participants and the audience. The focus of this discussion, then, is to help festival sponsors avoid the appearance of impropriety, thus maintaining the credibility of the festival and reducing the potential for controversy. By careful selection of adjudicators, contest organizers help to promote their own reputations as well as those of the adjudicators who serve them.

## Providing for Adjudicators

Once the festival organizers have selected adjudicators, their next step is to make proper arrangements for them. These arrangements may be so involved as to require travel, lodging, and food for the duration of the event. In addition, there are provisions that an adjudicator might expect or appreciate—copies of the scripts as appropriate, a properly equipped table or work area, and an orientation in which the sponsors share their expectations and adjudicators are free to ask questions for clarification.

While this requirement is controversial, it is also not universal. Some festivals require that adjudicators be provided with copies of the complete script as produced by festival participants. In such cases, festival sponsors provide scripts well enough in advance to allow the adjudicators time to read and study the plays to their own satisfaction. In these cases, giving scripts in advance, in addition to allowing for study of the script and getting to know it thoroughly prior to the adjudication, provides the opportunity for adjudicators to read what the playwright may have said about it. This expectation is more prevalent in the British system, but American festivals, most notably the American Association of Community Theatres, also engage in the practice of requiring scripts be advanced to the adjudicators.

## Work areas and seating arrangements

With or without advance copies of the scripts, adjudicators can reasonably expect that the festival sponsors will provide them with an adequate work area on site. The best such spaces are actual tables with detached seats, though sometimes adjudicators are provided with an auditorium seat and a portable lapboard or desk that can rest on the row in front of them. In either case, festival organizers should provide each adjudicator with his own light source, a set of scoring sheets with the identifying information completed in advance, a fresh pad of paper for written notes, and writing instruments—preferably both pencils and a pen so that the adjudicator can use the one with which he is most comfortable. Additional blank scoring sheets are also helpful in case of an error that requires an adjudicator to create a new form. Organizers should rope off these adjudicator workstations to prevent or severely limit public access. Workstations should be at least one-third to half-way back in the auditorium, and should have a clear view of the stage. Hosts should always provide drinking water. They may provide other refreshments should they so choose. Some sort of mint or lozenge to sooth the throat for speaking may be especially helpful, but if used, hosts should provide unwrapped items to avoid the sound of opening the wrappers.

Festival hosts should also provide a separate, dedicated and private space for the adjudicators to gather during scheduled breaks, performance delays, and to complete scoring sheets and make final decisions at the end of the event. Hosts should equip this site with snacks and refreshments. Many adjudicators appreciate coffee, especially in longer festival settings. If appropriate in the context of the festival schedule, this space would serve for providing meals to adjudicators.

## Reviewing expectations with adjudicators

Festival hosts should conduct a thorough orientation that helps adjudicators to understand what is expected of them, how the festival will operate, and what final awards or determinations rest with them. Adjudicators have the right to expect a dedicated time in the schedule for this orientation. During this time, the festival organizers should review the overall plan for the festival, the rules and guidelines of the event, the projected schedule, the scoring system, appropriate procedures for determining final outcomes, and a list of any rankings, ratings or awards that the adjudicators are to determine in the course of their work. Festival organizers are encouraged to provide as much information as possible during this orientation and, as allowed by rules of the festival, may choose to provide supplemental information to further adjudicators' efforts to fulfill their roles. Over the past several years, I have accumulated a page of supplemental information for adjudicators. The document addresses a variety of concerns that are not explicit in the existing festival rules, but in past contests, complicated matters because they were not part of the adjudicator orientation process. Topics include everything from when to expect lunch to how students tend to interpret numerical scores to the selection of an all-star cast to additional awards at the discretion of the judges. The items appear in no particular order, but the list is amended from year to year as new issues arise in the hosting of a contest or festival.

What standards of scoring do festival organizers expect from their adjudicators? This area is the core of the issue for festival participants and their directors. In my experience, organizers should always emphasize three areas of concern with adjudicators.

**1)** Individual scores and rankings, when they are used, must match one another. Only once in my history as a host institution for a play contest did I ever remove myself from the operation of the festival. I was competing in the event, and in an effort to avoid the appearance of impropriety, I asked a colleague familiar with the play contest format to coordinate the events on the day of the contest. I reviewed all of the procedures with my surrogate, made myself available to him for questions, and avoided all direct contact with the judges. As part of the contest documentation, I provided a summary page of results. The contest was over, the results announced, the adjudicators gone, and the students and directors on their way out of the building before one of the participating directors noticed that the summary sheet reflected that one of the judges had named the play he had given the second-highest score his first-place ranking. We first checked to make certain it was not a transposition error. It was not. It was a tight contest with a split decision, and if the scores, rather than the rankings, were accurate, it would change the outcome of the contest.

We convened all the directors who had participated in the contest, together with my colleague who ran the event. I apologized for the error, and accepted blame for not being explicit about the need to make certain that rankings and scores matched—I had never faced a situation like this one in the past. With all directors present, we contacted the offending judge by cell phone and, without explaining our reason for calling, asked him to clarify whether the highest score or the highest ranking was his vote for the first place production. His initial impulse was to challenge the expectation that rankings and scores should match, but he eventually provided the answer we needed to finalize the results of the contest.

I have since moved into full-time administration where I serve more often as host than as participant in play contests, but I have never again given up access to the operation of a festival for which I had responsibility. Instead, I always invited a fellow director to move with me through the process and the interaction with judges so that together we could attest to the integrity of the event. I have also made clear in the orientation that for each individual adjudicator, scores and rankings must match, and in a related concern, that no adjudicator may assign two different productions the same total score. Ties may occur through adding the rankings or scores of multiple judges, but may never appear in an individual judge's work.

**2)** A second area of concern that festival hosts should always address with adjudicators during the orientation is how students—especially secondary school students—interpret scores. The autonomy of the adjudicator is sacrosanct and inviolable. Each adjudicator has the right to score and rank a festival as he sees fit, but some adjudicators—particularly those from college ranks or community or professional theatre settings—do not realize how students react to scores. Many high school students attend schools with a 100-point grading system in which any grade below a 70 is a failing grade. In every festival I coordinate, I explain this concept to adjudicators, pointing out that if they want to communicate to the participating production team that they have failed in the efforts, a score below 70 is an excellent way to do so. I remind them that they have total autonomy over their individual scores, but respectfully ask them to consider establishing a minimum score of 70 for any individual production. This practice, while more easily implemented in smaller festivals, can be effectively used in larger ones as well—and it applies only to those competitive contests where numerical scores are used.

3) Festival adjudicators, at times, may find it appropriate to share some basic background information about festival participants—not to influence the outcome of the festival, but to help direct them in the delivery of oral critiques. When adjudicators do not know the background of a producing organization, it can sometimes be difficult for them to formulate a constructive, helpful critique. A fledgling school program with a young, inexperienced director may need a somewhat softer assessment with more encouragement than criticism in the evaluation. A veteran program with an exemplary track record, on the other hand, may benefit more from a direct, aggressive critique with a great deal of attention to detail.

The notion of sharing this information with adjudicators is not without controversy, and is probably only appropriate in non-competitive settings. Most adjudicators will discern the background of a program simply by watching their performance. But to the extent that sharing background information with adjudicators can enhance the educational value of the festival experience, festival organizers should at least consider the prospect.

Adjudicators, throughout the orientation process, should be free to interrupt with questions and to ask for clarification. Orientation is an important element of a smooth flowing and successful play festival.

## Remuneration for adjudicators

In their terms of engagement, the British Guild of Drama Adjudicators requires a minimum payment of £66 for public adjudication of one to three plays and a minimum of £20 for each additional play in a festival as a base rate for full members. Complications and additions of various kinds augment this basic fee with additional remuneration. The base rate converts to a little over $100 for an adjudicator to evaluate a festival of three productions, with an additional $33 for each play beyond three. While the base rate is probably on par with many American festivals and contests, the additional fee per play would quickly bust the budget of larger festivals. Regardless what models are used in its development, festival organizations have a responsibility to establish, and adjudicators have the right to expect, some sort of remuneration for sharing their expertise as an evaluator. The provision should include an honorarium for their service to the festival or contest, travel reimbursement, food and, if required, lodging for the event.

To give one example, the Georgia High School Association currently pays $100 plus food, lodging, and travel for judges at the state one-act play championship each fall. Region secretaries throughout the organization adhere to or improve on this format. Some regions with more than ten participants in the region actually provide an honorarium of $150 to $200 plus expenses. The Georgia Theatre Conference, which now sponsors two concurrent festivals at their annual convention, pays each adjudicator a base rate for the first ten plays, plus an additional fee for each additional play beyond ten. There are various approaches to recognizing the adjudicator with payment. Any approach is acceptable as long as it is communicated clearly to the adjudicators and they agree to the terms of engagement.

Whenever possible, the contest host should have the payment ready to share with the adjudicators when they complete their work and are ready to leave the festival site. Some organizations may require reimbursement forms or other information to process payment, but as a courtesy to the adjudicators, organizers should do whatever they can to expedite the payment.

By addressing these common concerns, festival hosts and organizers can make the adjudication experience as positive for the adjudicators as they hope it will be for the participants.

# CHAPTER EIGHT

## Training and Certifying Adjudicators

At the beginning of this book, I cited three broad goals for myself. I hoped to describe a model for oral and written production critiques in festival or competition settings. I wanted readers to understand that the role of the adjudicator is to make adjudication a positive and powerful experience in the life of theatre students. I wanted to inspire readers to strive to be respected in their critiques of theatre productions. I said that I did not want to complain about judging—I wanted to do something about it. In the early 1990s via workshops with James Dodding at the annual convention of the Southeastern Theatre Conference, and more recently at state conventions in Georgia and Mississippi, I have tried to do just that. In this chapter, I propose a simple, three-step process for training adjudicators, and suggest a model for adjudicator certification and recertification on an annual or biennial basis.


### Step One: Orientation

Trainees begin the process with a general orientation session that briefly introduces many of the basic tenets described in this work. The session introduces participants to the British adjudication model, and the professional responsibilities and moral obligations of adjudicators, with extended discussion of the aesthetic distance required to enable adjudicators to deliver an honest assessment of the theatre performance in the least threatening manner. The trainer reviews the plan for the remaining sessions, and invites anyone who wants to receive a certificate of completion to attend and participate in the remaining sessions. Participants interested in completing the program review the performance schedule and select a production to attend and critique.

## Step Two: Attending a Performance

The second session of the training process involves attending a production. Ideally, all participants in the workshop will attend the same performance. By seeing the same production, the novice adjudicators will learn from listening to one another and comparing their personal observations to the observations of their colleagues. When it is not possible for everyone to attend the same production, participants may still continue the process and complete the requirements for certification. They simply do not share one of the common experiences that help to make the training process greater than the sum of its parts.

Either during or after the performance, participants complete written notes that they will later use to formulate and deliver an oral critique of the production. They receive a template with a suggested format inspired by the British adjudication model, for recording observations. Approaches to note taking vary widely among trainees, and there is no "right" or "wrong" answer. Ultimately, adjudicators are encouraged to develop a personal approach that works for them. They should maintain a consistent structure in future settings where they respond to more than one production.

When scheduling allows for it, the participants will have a significant break between the second and third sessions of the training to give them time to reflect on the productions, consider their observations, and develop their written and oral critiques.

## Step Three: Delivering an Oral Critique and Receiving Feedback

The third component of the training process occurs after trainees have attended a performance and recorded their thoughts, reactions, and observations. Each trainee delivers his commentary in front of the group. Each is encouraged to follow the rubric provided in the training as a means of ensuring all production elements are included in the commentary.

While each trainee delivers his presentation, the trainer completes a rubric evaluating the adjudicator. Immediately after each oral adjudication, the trainer comments on the adjudicator's performance. Both of these oral presentations are formal in nature, incorporating the principals of formal adjudication as presented earlier.

This cycle of trainee's oral critique and trainer's commentary continues until all participants in the training program have presented and received oral feedback, making it the most unpredictable, and likely the longest, of the three sessions. After commenting on the adjudicator's delivery, the trainer gives the completed evaluation rubric to the trainee for review and future reference. At the end of this session, students who finish all three components receive a certificate of completion. Examples of both the play adjudication worksheet and the evaluation of adjudicator are found on the following two pages.

## PLAY ADJUDICATION WORKSHEET

---

**Stage Presentation** (10 points)—*Address each element of stage presentation*

Stage setting:
Props
Lighting
Costumes
Makeup
Effects/Other

*Additional comments*

---

**Production** (35 points)—*Address the overall impact of the production as a whole*

Was spirit and meaning of the play adequately interpreted?
Team work
General pace and variations in tempo
Grouping/Stage pictures
Movement
Dramatic build

*Additional comments*

---

**Acting** (40 points)—*Address the work of every actor in the production, individually or collectively*

Characterization
Projection & Diction
Variation in Tone & Emphasis/Expression
Gesture/Movement

*Additional comments*

---

**Endeavor/Originality/General Attainment** (15 points)—*Address the dramatic value of the production*

General impression made by the performance
Type of play
Degree of difficulty
Dramatic merit
Suitability for cast

---

                                        **TOTAL POINTS _____**

**Adjudicator
Signature:**_____
**Date:**_____

## EVALUATION OF ADJUDICATOR

NAME:_____

PLAY:_____

### I. TECHNICAL

    A. Knowledge of Subject
    B. Specific Comments presented
    C. Adequate coverage of
        1. Presentation (Technical)
        2. Production
        3. Technical
        4. Impact (Endeavor)

### II. MANNER

    A. Platform Presence
    B. Eye Contact
    C. Rapport with Audience
    D. Voice
    E. Vocabulary

### III. APPEARANCE

    A. Clothes
    B. Stance
    C. Other

### IV. GENERAL COMMENTS

    A. Was I interested?
    B. Were comments arranged logically?
    C. Did I learn something?
    D. Was I excited? Stimulated? Bored? Confused? Offended?
    E. Did the adjudicator's presentation mar the enjoyment of the
       audience?
    F. Other

### V. SUGGESTIONS FOR DEVELOPMENT/SUMMARY REMARKS

*Signature:*_____ *Date:*_____

*"Would I respect this adjudicator?"*

**Mandating Certification: A Bridge Too Far**

When I worked with James Dodding to introduce this model for adjudicator training, I saw a tremendous opportunity to have a positive impact on the operation of festivals and competitions across the Southeast and in my home state. I did not foresee the reactions that came from friends and colleagues in the field. My suggestion that we move to a system that required certification for adjudicators prompted rather harsh resistance, resentment, and complaints, mostly from veteran educators who had been adjudicating plays for two decades or more. A young upstart who set out to change the world was trying to tell veteran adjudicators—some of whom had been judging plays since before he was born—that they suddenly needed to go through a training program to be certified to evaluate theatre performances. The resisters had a point, of course, but I didn't understand that at the time.

My strategy to pursue adjudicator certification had been a top-down approach with organizations such as Georgia High School Association, Southeastern Theatre Conference, Georgia Theatre Conference and others mandating the certification process and allowing only certified adjudicators to participate in their events. This policy would force everyone into adjudicator training programs.

My first effort to effect change came in my home state of Georgia. I worked my connections with the Georgia Theatre Conference, and the Georgia Chapter of the International Thespian Society, but I quickly ran into a wall of resistance. By the time I realized the arrogance of my personal crusade, I suggested a grandfather clause that would exempt veteran adjudicators from certification requirements, but the damage was done. I took my idea back into my cave and nursed my wounds. The adjudicator training program was dormant for the next several years.

A few years ago, I was asked by members of the Board of Directors of the Georgia Theatre Conference to offer my adjudicator training workshop at their annual convention in October. After a hiatus of nearly a decade, I dusted off my notes and conducted the sessions. I have offered the program on an annual basis every year since. I also had the privilege of doing the training workshops for the Mississippi Theatre Association in 2007.

My second effort to introduce adjudicator training was more effective and more successful because it was a grassroots effort. Instead of trying to impose my will on others, my approach was simply to provide an opportunity for anyone who wanted to become a better adjudicator to do so by participating in our workshops. I have conducted the training sessions with as many as twenty and as few as four participants. Some participants do not complete the program, but if they attend only the orientation session, they still gain valuable information that can improve their efforts in adjudication.

### Looking to the Future: A Plan for Recertification?

If we establish a tradition of certified adjudicators, then at some point in the future we will need to consider some sort of renewal or recertification process. A recertification process for adjudicator training is probably not an immediate concern, but an annual or biennial plan would help to address two areas of need. First, a retraining would keep adjudicators informed and up to date about changes in organizational rules and procedures in the state. Second, the training experience would encourage practicing adjudicators to engage in an honest self-assessment, reviewing core principles laid out in the original training.

The recertification process would be modeled after the three-step training program. The first session would involve a review of basic principles of adjudication, and a review of festival rules from various festival hosts in the state. The second and third sessions would then run in the same format as the original training, with candidates for recertification seeing a performance, delivering an oral critique and receiving immediate feedback.

## Qualifications for Trainers

If the discipline of adjudication evolves into a profession, the shift will include training and certification as well as practices and procedures that require and enforce high expectations from practitioners. The question arises—who does the training?

An effective trainer would have a track record of success in adjudicating festivals and competitions, a reputation for professionalism, and a commitment to the philosophy of adjudication reflected by practicing adjudicators. A trainer should have positive references and recommendations, as well as a history of being invited to return. When a potential trainer has participated in a festival with a formal evaluation process for adjudicators, those evaluations should be made available for review.

At first glance, a successful record may seem to be the equivalent of a reputation for professionalism, but in the field of adjudication there are successful adjudicators who do not possess this reputation. A popular culture analogy may be found in television talent programs where a panel of adjudicators (often with the help of the viewing audience) determines the fate of the performers. It is easy to understand that all of the adjudicators in these programs have a successful track record, but not all are recognized for their professional conduct in the role. Some, in fact, play the role of antihero, a hurdle that the competitor must jump to move forward. Reputation is best assessed by listening to what audience and participants say about an individual's adjudication.

Finally, a trainer must be ready to commit to the philosophy of adjudicator training, certification, and recertification. The role will come with considerable authority, but also with equal or greater responsibilities. Trainers may have to share difficult commentary with adjudicators about their work, or even face situations where desired certification is not awarded. While these kinds of concerns may not occur early in the development of adjudicator training programs, once a standard is introduced, concerns, questions and controversies about maintaining the standard are sure to arise. Adjudicator trainers must assume the burden of policing the people with whom they work.

**Evaluating the Evaluators**

Any effective effort to improve the adjudication experience and offer formal training to adjudicators must include evaluation. In other arts, music festivals have advanced well beyond the theatre discipline in evaluating judges, but many theatre festivals include a means of adjudicator evaluation. Two notable organizations that have adopted a process to facilitate evaluation include the Florida Thespians and the American Association of Community Theatre.

The Florida Thespian organization provides a standard form that troupe sponsors can use to submit recommendations concerning judges who adjudicate in one-act play or individual events at their annual conference. The evaluation sheet begins with the comment, "In light of the adjudication given at the festival, I should like to submit the following:"

The evaluation includes the judge's name or number, and details of the adjudication being evaluated—category, location, date, and other pertinent details. The evaluator is then asked to respond to these four statements by assigning ratings of "fair," "good," "excellent" and "superior." Each statement appears below:

*1. The adjudicator was able to communicate with my student(s) and explain the problems in a well written manner.*

*2. The adjudicator gave my student(s) constructive criticism and offered solutions.*

*3. The adjudicator seems aware of the theatrical process as it applies to high-school-age students.*

*4. The adjudicator was alert and an active participant in the adjudication process.*

The evaluator then is given the opportunity to make additional comments, and is asked to "highly recommend" this judge be either "retained" or "dismissed." The evaluator includes his name and troupe information as part of the process.

The American Association of Community Theatre (AACT) implements a formal adjudicator evaluation process into their festivals. Prior to the first performance, the Festival Chair provides Adjudicator Evaluation forms to a representative from each company presenting at the festival, and at least five festival attendees who are willing to complete the evaluation and agree to see at least 80% of the performances and their respective adjudications. The evaluation form opens with a comment similar to the one used in the Florida Thespian Conference.

"Given the conditions under which the adjudication was delivered, please rate the adjudicator on the following criteria. Additional comments are encouraged and should be written on the back side."

The core of the evaluation asks the evaluator to assign the adjudicator a rating of "outstanding," "very good," "good," "fair" or "poor" on eight areas of concern. The evaluator assesses to what extent the adjudicator:

– *Focused on the producing group, acknowledging its dignity and capability.*

– *Effectively communicated by establishing an appropriate rapport.*

– *Was open-minded, honest, and responsive to the group's work.*

– *Was knowledgeable and provided accurate, critically relevant responses.*

– *Opened up new awareness and alternative possibilities in a constructive manner.*

*– Was clear, thorough, and appropriately specific.*

*– Showed an understanding of community theatre.*

*– Adhered to criteria as outlined in the Handbook.*

Evaluators are asked if they are affiliated with a company participating in the festival, and if they would want the individual they are evaluating to adjudicate at another festival. If they answer "no" to this last question, they are asked to explain their reasons on the back of the form.

The evaluator includes his name, telephone number, and email address, and signs a statement to certify that he saw and heard at least 80% of the adjudicator's responses for the festival.

Evaluation forms are completed and returned to the Festival Commission Representative before the awards announcement. The Festival Chair sends the forms to the AACT office immediately following the festival. Information identifying the evaluator is redacted, and adjudicators receive copies of the evaluation(s) to help direct them in improving their skills.

An effective adjudicator-training program can improve theatre festivals and contests, but may also have implications beyond the festival setting. The process, in effect, promotes critical thinking and addresses a number of ethical considerations in how to communicate with one another. These skills are valuable to more than just theatre artists or artists in general. Creative and critical thought is a valuable commodity across the disciplines.

# CHAPTER NINE

## The Good, the Bad and the Ugly:
## Actual Adjudicator Comments

Adjudicators have power. They have the power to build up and encourage others, to improve the quality of the lives of those whom they serve. They also have the power to destroy, discourage, and demean the same population. Much of the content of this book has come from personal experience over the past quarter of a century. I have delivered play critiques. I have subjected my work, both as an actor and a director, to the whims and fancies of adjudicators in festivals and competitions. I have watched hundreds of adjudicators respond to plays that I have seen. Some impressed me. Others entertained me. Still others annoyed me, and a few offended me. Many left something in their wake—a written commentary, their personal thoughts and observations. I dedicate this chapter of the text to the power and the legacy of the adjudicator by sharing the good, the bad, and the ugly highlights from actual adjudicator comments, collected from friends, colleagues, and personal experience.

### The Good

Good comments can be good for a number of reasons. Some are good because of the detail, others because of the new concepts or alternate perspectives they offer, and still others because—well, just because they make us feel good. The following list of adjudicator observations fall into the category that I would label "good" commentary. This label does not mean that the comments said only good things about the performance, but constructively critical observations were given with a level of specificity that enables the director and production team to leave with a positive learning experience.

"A farce *must* be overdone."

"I wish the various people had used the spoon to stir and taste the soup; it would have been more consistent."

"Train platform groups were a bit too linear."

"After the revolver dialogue, the two young men need to exit with purpose."

"I commend you on inclusion of so many in the team effort."

"Challenging play, bold, courageous endeavor."

"Petruchio—don't let your character voice and too-brisk pacing spoil your interpretation…diction is critical in Shakespeare."

"Really have to commend you for taking on Shakespeare—and doing a fine job with him."

"Like Algernon—he's wonderfully over the top and Earnest/Jack does a nice job of matching him quite often."

"Did a very nice job of ensemble acting—and a very nice job of catching the rather tipsy flavor of Wilde's play."

"Changes in moods were effective for the most part—a very strong ensemble—you worked well together."

"At times the production was so involved I was amazed I didn't get distracted."

"Moving…I could feel your passion, I could see you out there on the battle field."

"Accents are difficult, especially with the full cast—15 or so of you—trying them. I appreciate that yours were consistent across the board. And you kept the dialogue clear and understandable in spite of the overlaid dialect work. Mama, I especially loved your vocal variety and expressive voice. It was melodious. Way to go. Way to go all of you."

## The Bad

Bad commentary, like good, can come into being for a variety of reasons. Perhaps a lack of specificity is among the major causes of bad comments. Observations that are unclear, that do not communicate a point effectively, also constitute bad commentary. If good commentary teaches, bad commentary does not. As you review the list of highlights I offer as examples of bad commentary, consider the level of detail the adjudicator provided. If you were the actor or director to whom it was addressed, what you would learn from the experience?

"Where did you get the wonderful little boy?"

"Watch extraneous movements that don't add to the characterization."

"Blind lady was impressive."

"Your emotion is confusing in your delivery of lines after death of your son."

"Some lines sounded memorized."

"Some nice facial expressions."

"Great voice and presence…great entrance…great energy…great chemistry…great picturization."

"The actor had good pace and energy and timing."

"It's okay for a dramatic piece to be slower paced than a musical, but…"

"Missed message."

"Great job! Great coordination and great cast to pull off such a great production…Lead actor was great—Good luck—Great job!"

My personal favorite comes from our production of John Guare's *A Few Stout Individuals*. Over the years our school had developed a reputation for strong male performers, not always common in public high schools. Adjudicators would fairly often comment on having so many strong men in our shows, but this particular adjudicator spoke from a perspective I had never heard before.

"Wow, you sure can grow facial hair where you're from!"

## And, the Ugly

We have all said it in reference to personal or professional moments in our lives where someone said or did something that was just beyond the pale. The most distressing thing about these ugly highlights is that all of the comments were actually made—many in the adjudicator's own handwriting.

"Well, that was unnecessary!"

"Play drags to a dirge."

"Is there a reason for the set?"

"This is what I call a talking-heads play. Movement and action are scarce."

"This didn't happen."

"I just didn't BELIEVE you."

"They should have been sitting in the audience with me, only then would they have realized why I was wincing the entire performance."

And so it goes. All of these examples came from well-informed, well-intentioned, and fundamentally honest adjudicators whose heartfelt desire was to encourage theatre, and yet the responses are so very different. They are all very much the same in one respect—they illustrate the power and the influence of the voice of the adjudicator. Ten and twenty years later we still talk about the moments when we submitted our work for someone else to critique. The comments of these individuals help to shape the fabric of our memories, and the nature of our response to growth in the pursuit of art.

# CHAPTER TEN

## Creating the Critical Thinker:
## A Broader Perspective for Adjudicator Training

Training for adjudicators need not be limited to regional and state theatre festivals, but should arguably be a part of the training for every artist and educator in theatre—perhaps even in every arts discipline. In his text *The Essential Theatre*, Oscar Brockett included a discussion of the value of art I regularly use when I teach a college introductory theatre course. He suggested that ultimately the value of any art form is determined by its ability to enhance the quality of life "by increasing our sensitivity to others and our surroundings, by sharpening our perceptions, by reshaping our values so that moral and societal concerns take precedence over materialistic goals." As I teach non-majors in the college setting, one of my goals is to help students learn to assess the value of art in their own lives by establishing the metrics by which they can measure aesthetic value and enabling them to develop and articulate their own systems of evaluation. These discussions always begin with the quote from Brockett. During the past few semesters, I have introduced the adjudicator training process described in this chapter as a means of teaching students how to think critically when evaluating the performance of a play. The use of a rubric in the training process is a major component of many education reform initiatives because it helps the student understand what it is that he is supposed to learn from the experience or course. The rubric, though, has a second value. It provides students with a sample framework for critical thinking. Once students comprehend

and implement such a framework, they become more familiar with the structure of assessment, enabling them to assess
in other areas, adapting and modifying the structure as
needed. The process of critical thinking is very much like
riding a bicycle or climbing a ladder. First, you need to
understand the structure of the item—how it works.
Initially, the rider or climber might be awkward and unco-
ordinated, but over a period of time mental and motor skills
begin to work together and the movements become more
fluid, more precise, and more automatic than in the early
stages of learning. The rider or climber eventually becomes
quite adept at riding—or climbing. After an extended
period of time—a year, perhaps—without engaging in the
physical activity, the performers may experience an awkward moment or two, but more often than not can quickly
resume the movements without serious difficulty unless
they have suffered some physical or mental impairment
since the time they first learned the process. I contend that a
similar path can be taken in the teaching of critical thinking
skills, except in this case the experience takes students even
further in their development as human beings.

The similarity comes in the instructional process itself.
Using the adjudicator training model as an example, students are introduced to the activity through an orientation
process that ultimately provides them with a rubric for
evaluating the performance of a play. This first step introduces students to the structure of the tool they will be
using. The trainer takes them through guided practice
activities, not unlike the use of training wheels, or that
moment in a bike rider's life when his parent walks or runs
alongside, holding him steady. Eventually, the students step
out on their own—as the trainer lets go and becomes an
observer and responder rather than a teacher. Before long,
students take the rudimentary skills they learned and begin

to build on them, eventually performing feats that the original trainer never even dreamed of, let alone was able to do—as when the biker can pop wheelies, stand, or ride with no hands. With an understanding of the structure and nature of critical thinking, students have the opportunity to excel beyond the imagination of their teachers, and this concept is where the metaphor parts from the original motor skills of the biking example. The first produces skilled—even creative—technicians who know how to do what can be done. The second produces in the minds of the students a way of seeing and experiencing life that is able to imagine how to do what *cannot* be done.

Another model I like to use for assessing and articulating aesthetic value is found in Goethe's three questions. Recognized as one of the greatest figures in Western literature, German poet, novelist, playwright, courtier, and natural philosopher Johann Wolfgang von Goethe (1749-1832), suggested that one can assess art by asking, in order, three basic questions:

1. What was the artist trying to achieve?

2. Was he successful in achieving it?

3. Was it worth the effort?

Goethe suggested that the questions should be addressed in order; there is no reason to respond to the third question until the first two have been answered. Because they provide an alternate set of criteria by which an observer can assess the value of a work of art, Goethe's questions further expand the perspective and vocabulary of the potential adjudicator.

Both the Brockett and the Goethe models are designed to assess the value of art. Adjudication in general, and especially in certain settings, is not intended to pass judgment on a production but rather to provide an honest response and assessment of the effectiveness of the performance. The value of these models to adjudicator training, then, is found in their ability to expand the vocabulary, provide sample structures, and influence the mindset of the adjudicator trainee. The concepts of Brockett and Goethe help the adjudicator move from "I was moved by your performance," to "I was moved by your performance because..." In other words, the application of these ideas enables the adjudicator to respond more meaningfully to the theatre endeavor. Whether by using Brockett, Goethe, another historical source, or their own philosophy, conscientious, well-trained adjudicators would be well advised to consider their options and identify the means and structure by which they will make their observations.

## Developing Critical Thinking Skills

In the midst of the current accountability issues in education, the ability to use theatre adjudication as a means of developing critical thinking skills has huge implications. Fifty years of concern about falling test scores in math and science have prompted policy makers to require more and harder math and science. Because the raising of the bar in this manner ignored the fact that many students were struggling with the rudimentary skills necessary to engage in advanced work, the result was to further drive down scores, creating more concern and resulting in still more added expectations. In a recent conversation, a career educator observed that most of our students are trying to learn math they will *never* use. While I recognize the hyperbole in his statement, I also see the truth in his observation. In order to use the math they learn, they need to be able to imagine how they might be able to use it, how they might want to use it, and how it might bring them benefit. The critical thinking process enables students to use what they have experienced in order to speculate, imagine, and respond to things or ideas they come across that they have not experienced. This same process also enables students to use their imaginations to envision what no one has experienced. Creativity is what brings excitement to education and energy into the lives of students, and that creativity comes from engaging in the experience of *thinking*.

The adjudication process as a means of promoting critical thinking skills should not be limited to theatre students or even to arts students. We need to expose *all* students to the process early and often, offer professional development courses for classroom teachers, and introduce the format as a regular component of college theatre courses and other courses in aesthetics—but who will do the training? Theatre professionals with a background in this comprehensive, holistic approach to assessment will "train the trainers."

If, as a reader, you think I have gone a little overboard here, consider the world in which we live. When I was a child we purchased a 23-volume set of encyclopedias so that I could have access to all the information in the world. Today, that information, and inconceivably more, hangs from a lanyard around my neck in a piece of hardware smaller than my finger. When I was a child, the purpose of education was to teach children information. Today, the purpose of education is to teach children how to find information. When I was a child, I learned how to solve problems. Today, too many students learn only how to compute formulas, which is why our students struggle so much with basic word

problems in math or simple reading comprehension problems in a language arts course. Each of these differences is
the result of entering into the digital age. Digitalization is a
wonderful tool. It has and will continue to serve mankind in
unbelievable ways, but it is only a tool. The human experience is a verbal experience. It is a relational experience. It
is an experience that manifests itself not through numbers,
test scores, or statistics, but through creative thought and
the spoken and written word.

The human experience—the human journey—is what
inspired me to write this book in the first place. If my goal
at the beginning of the journey was to make a difference,
then my best chance to have a positive impact rests with
you, the reader. I hope you will take the concepts discussed
in this book with you on *your* journey, adding them to your
experience and your wisdom as you respond to the works
of others.